Peter Fullagar

Peter Fullagar was raised in Kent and studied for a BA (Hons) in English and Sociology at Anglia Ruskin University in Cambridge, before going on to complete an MA in English Language and Literature at the University of Westminster.

He is a writer and editor of educational materials for the English language industry and formerly worked as an English teacher in Tokyo, Moscow and London.

He lives in Berkshire with his partner.

www.peterjfullagar.co.uk

First published in the U.K. in 2022 by Aurora Metro Publications Ltd, 80
Hill Rise, Richmond, TW10 6UB UK

www.aurorametro.com info@aurorametro.com

Virginia Woolf in Richmond © 2018 Peter Fullagar hardback edition

Virginia Woolf in Richmond © 2022 Peter Fullagar paperback edition

Editor: Cheryl Robson

Cover design © 2018 Scarlett Rickard

ISBN 978-1-912430-80-2

Printed by Short Run Press, Exeter on sustainably resourced paper.

VIRGINIA WOOLF
in
RICHMOND

written and selected by
Peter Fullagar

AURORA METRO BOOKS

Contents

Acknowledgements

The author would like to thank all those who made this book possible, especially The Society of Authors, Sussex University, Penguin Random House and Houghton Mifflin Harcourt for permission to include extracts from the published works of both Virginia and Leonard Woolf.

I'm grateful too for invaluable mentoring from Cheryl Robson at Aurora Metro and to Ferroccio, Angie and Piers for your support and encouragement. Special thanks must go to Paula Maggio for writing the foreword as well as Emma Woolf for her input and inspiration.

Thanks also to my family and friends for your support through the writing of this book, which is dedicated to my father, Gordon Fullagar (1942-2017).

Foreword

by Paula Maggio

Richmond often fails to get the respect it deserves from Virginia Woolf scholars and readers. You won't find it in the index of *Virginia Woolf A to Z* by Mark Hussey, the premiere reference book for Woolf scholars. You will hear it characterized as a place Woolf disliked. And if you made a pilgrimage to the very Richmond building where Virginia and Leonard lived the longest – Hogarth House, located at 24 Paradise Road – you may have failed to notice it at all. I made that trip from London on an overcast, rainy day in June 2016, meeting Emma Woolf, great-niece of the literary couple, in a small café across the street from the Richmond train station. Ironically, Virginia's famous quote used by many food establishments and food writers – 'One cannot think well, love well, sleep well, if one has not dined well' – decorated the main wall of the café, suggesting a connection to Virginia but not explaining it. From the café, Emma and I embarked on a brief walking tour of Richmond. When we arrived at Hogarth House, we were chagrined to see that it was suffering from neglect. A thick overgrown vine covered much of the building's front exterior at the ground level, almost completely obscuring the blue plaque marking it as an historic site where the couple lived from 1915-1924 and where they founded the Hogarth Press. Unpainted plywood covered the main entrance and its sidelights.

A large sign with a colorful list of "Site Safety" cautions was prominently affixed to the front door of the Georgian brick home, warning visitors away.

Since then, some things have changed. In the fall of 2017, realtors put a refurbished Hogarth House on the market at a price of £4.4 million, garnering it much publicity as the Woolfs' former home. Photos showed a pristine entryway set off by four glossy white pillars, with the formerly overgrown vine now neatly trained around windows and along the black wrought iron fence. It no longer obscured the historic blue plaque. Around that same time, a local arts charity, Aurora Metro, began promoting its campaign to erect a life-sized full figure statue of Virginia Woolf seated on a bench on Richmond Riverside and to raise £50,000 to fund its cost. Fittingly, the piece by acclaimed sculptor Laury Dizengremel is meant to recognize the ten years Virginia spent in Richmond.

Dizengremel's sculpture also pays homage to the work Virginia completed there, as well as Richmond's appearance in her later fiction. While living in Richmond, Virginia wrote countless reviews and essays, along with such fiction as *Two Stories* (1917), *Kew Gardens* (1919), *Night and Day* (1919), *Monday or Tuesday* (1921), and *Jacob's Room* (1922). Richmond also figured as a location in her later writing as well.

Virginia Woolf in Richmond by Peter Fullagar, is a timely companion piece to this recent recognition – of Richmond in general and Hogarth House in particular – as locations important to Virginia and her writing. As a writer and editor who is a member of the Virginia Woolf statue campaign and someone who has reported on the effort for HuffPost UK, Fullagar is ideally positioned to make the case for Richmond's importance in Virginia's life and work. He does just that in *Virginia Woolf in Richmond*, providing a comprehensive analysis of the time Virginia spent in the suburb, a mere fifteen-minute train ride from central London. By mining Virginia's diaries and letters – rich resources always ready to reveal new insights into her inner and outer life as well as her work – Fullagar explores how living in the town influenced Virginia's life and her development as a writer.

He starts out by putting the lie to the negative quote about Richmond attributed to Virginia in the 2002 film *The Hours,* based on Michael Cunningham's 1998 novel by the same title. Fullagar shows us that discerning Virginia's true feelings about Richmond requires that one explore quotes garnered from her personal work. He leads us on that journey, quoting from Virginia's diaries and letters to convey her feelings – overwhelmingly positive – about Richmond itself, Hogarth House in particular, and living, working, and writing in Richmond, whose 'simplicities and refinements' she extolled in a 5 February 1921 letter to Violet Dickinson.

Drawing from her personal writing, Fullagar describes Virginia's life in the community – from her work with the Women's Co-operative Guild to her efforts to set up a bread shop to her long walks around town and country. Her 23 January 1918 diary entry, which Fullagar includes, aptly conveys her positive feelings about the Richmond countryside: 'We have glimpses of Heaven. So mild that the landing window is open, and I sat by the river watching a boat launched, and half expected to see buds on the willows'. Virginia was inordinately fond of Hogarth House, which the Woolfs made their home from March of 1915 through March of 1924. In her letters and diaries, she describes it as 'a perfect house, if ever there was one,' 'far the nicest house in England', and a 'beautiful and lovable house, which has done us such a good turn for almost precisely nine years'.

While biographies of Virginia recount the factual details of Hogarth Press history, this book does more. It explores the challenges and joys the Woolfs experienced in their day-to-day operations of the press. By quoting Virginia's diaries and letters, as well as Leonard's multi-volume autobiography, Fullagar conveys the couple's feelings about their endeavor over the years, from the Hogarth Press's 'very awkward beginning . . . in this very room, on this very green carpet', to its beanstalk-like growth, to its 1924 stature as a well-established and successful literary and commercial enterprise that had printed about 32 books during its years in Richmond.

Virginia Woolf in Richmond doesn't stop with the Hogarth Press. It goes on to mine Virginia's diaries and letters to help us understand her views on and experiences with writing, servants, family, leisure, and the Great War during the ten years she spent in Richmond. Scholars recognize the fact that the diaries and letters Virginia left behind are extraordinary resources that provide us with much territory still to explore on many topics. What Fullagar does in this book is give Virginia's years in Richmond their due. By carefully focusing on Virginia's own words written during that time period, he successfully argues that living in Richmond was an important and positive experience for this twentieth-century writer by showing how Richmond shaped Virginia's life and work. Including Leonard's thoughts about that time in their life reinforces its value. Indeed, Fullagar makes the case that Virginia left a rich and lasting literary legacy for Richmond, one that has yet to be duly recognized.

This book, published in association with the campaign to erect the first, full figure, life-size bronze statue of Virginia Woolf in Richmond, in celebration of the ten years that Virginia and Leonard lived there, gives recognition of that legacy a well-deserved boost.

*"I ought to be grateful to Richmond & Hogarth,
and indeed, whether it's my invincible optimism or not,
I am grateful."*

– Virginia Woolf

Chronology

1878 Leslie Stephen and Julia Duckworth marriage.

1879 [30 May] Vanessa Stephen born.

1880 [8 September] Julian Thoby Stephen born.
      [25 November] Leonard Woolf born.

1882 [25 January] Adeline Virginia Stephen born.

1883 [27 October] Adrian Leslie Stephen born.

1895 [5 May] Julia Stephen dies. Virginia has first
      breakdown.

1897 [10 April] Half-sister Stella Duckworth marriage.
      [19 July] Stella dies.

1904 [22 February] Leslie Stephen dies. Virginia's second
      breakdown. Stephen siblings move to 46 Gordon
      Square, Bloomsbury.
      [October] Leonard Woolf moves to Ceylon to work
      for Ceylon Civil Service.

1905 Beginning meetings of 'The Bloomsbury Group'.

1906 [September] Vanessa and Thoby ill on return from
      Greece.
      [20 November] Thoby dies. [22 November] Vanessa
      agrees to marry Clive Bell.

1907 [7 February] Vanessa and Clive Bell marriage.
      [April] Virginia and Adrian move to 29 Fitzroy
      Square.

1908 [4 February] Son of Vanessa, Julian Bell born.

1909 [17 February] Lytton Strachey proposes to Virginia,
      but retracts.

1910 [10 August] Son of Vanessa, Quentin Bell born.

1911 [May] Leonard Woolf returns from Ceylon on leave. Virginia moves to 38 Brunswick Square with Adrian, Duncan Grant, Maynard Keynes and Leonard Woolf.

1912 [January] Leonard proposes to Virginia. [February to March] Virginia has period of mental instability. [20 May] Leonard Woolf resigns from Civil Service.
[29 May] Virginia accepts Leonard's proposal.
[10 August] Virginia and Leonard Woolf marriage.

1913 Virginia has serious breakdown in summer. [9 September] Virginia attempts suicide.

1914 [4 August] War declared. [16 October] Virginia and Leonard rent rooms at 17 The Green, Richmond. Virginia and Leonard view Hogarth House towards the end of the year.

1915 [March] Leonard acquires lease for Hogarth House; Virginia's mental health deteriorates; *The Voyage Out* published.

1917 [April] Printing press arrives at Hogarth House. *Two Stories* published by Virginia and Leonard.

1918 [11 November] Armistice Day. [25 December] Daughter of Vanessa, Angelica Bell, born.

1919 [May] *Kew Gardens* published by Hogarth Press. [1 September] Virginia and Leonard take possession of Monk's House, Rodmell. [October] *Night and Day* published.

1922 [October] *Jacob's Room* published.

1924 [March] Virginia and Leonard move from Hogarth House to 52 Tavistock Square.

1925 [April] *The Common Reader* published. [May] *Mrs Dalloway* published.

1927 [May] *To the Lighthouse* published.

1928 [October] *Orlando* published. Virginia speaks at women's colleges in Cambridge.

1929 [October] *A Room of One's Own* published.

1931 [October] *The Waves* published.

1932 [21 January] Death of Lytton Strachey.

1933 [October] *Flush* published.

1934 [9 September] Death of Roger Fry.

1936 [April] After finishing *The Years*, Virginia collapses.

1937 [March] *The Years* published. [18 July] Death of Julian Bell.

1938 [June] *Three Guineas* published.

1939 [3 September] War on Germany declared.

1940 [July] *Roger Fry: A Biography* published.

1941 *Between the Acts* finished. [March] Virginia becomes ill.
[28 March] Virginia drowns herself in River Ouse. [18 April] Virginia's body found. [21 April] Virginia Woolf cremated.

1953 *A Writer's Diary* published.

1961 [7 April] Death of Vanessa Bell.

1969 [14 August] Death of Leonard Woolf.

1975 First edition of *Letters of Virginia Woolf* published; 6 volumes, 1975-1980.

1976 *Moments of Being* published.

1977 First edition of *The Diary of Virginia Woolf* published; 5 volumes, 1977-1984.

2017 The Hogarth Press celebrates centenary with publication of *Two Stories* by Virginia Woolf and Mark Haddon.

Introduction

*All the rooms, even when we first saw them in the dirty, dusty
desolation of an empty house, had beauty, repose, peace and
yet life.*

– Leonard Woolf

Why Richmond?

Virginia Woolf, aged 32, was an aspiring writer who had
recently completed her first novel when she moved to
Richmond, in south-west London. Leonard Woolf, her
husband, wanted to find somewhere quiet where Virginia
could fully recover her mental health, as the strain of writing
her debut novel, *The Voyage Out* had led to mental exhaustion
and collapse. Central London was considered too busy,
too full of distractions and social gatherings that could be
detrimental to Virginia's fragile state of mind, and so after
considering Hampstead and Twickenham, Richmond was
chosen as the ideal place for Virginia to reside. It was also
close to the nursing home, Burley House, in Twickenham,
where Virginia had been confined during her recent illness.

In October 1914, the couple first moved to a lodging
house on The Green in Richmond. The Woolfs were pacifists
and opposed to the war with Germany, but the reality of
the conflict would have been inescapable, due to the large

military presence in the town, with regular drills carried out at 8pm every evening on Richmond Green right opposite their lodgings. The town's small population swelled with hundreds of Belgian refugees and troops moving through the town to the Front.

While renting rooms with their Belgian landlady, Mrs le Grys at 17 The Green, the couple spotted Hogarth House, which was only a few minutes' walk away along Paradise Road. The Woolfs immediately fell in love with Hogarth House and set about acquiring it. They moved into the house in 1915, albeit under the dark shadow of Virginia's struggle to get well and the on-going stress of what was referred to initially as the 'European Crisis'. People had hoped the war would be over quickly but the food rationing and mounting number of casualties led to widespread distress. There was a Relief Committee to help those who were unemployed or widowed, while wounded soldiers were returning in large numbers to be nursed in Richmond Hospital and the military hospital which was created at the Star and Garter hotel. By May 1915, when the first Zeppelin airship bombing raids began over central London, the Third Battalion Signallers from the London Scottish Regiment were encamped in Richmond Park. In 1916, a new military hospital for South African soldiers was being built to house the hundreds of wounded survivors being transported to the town.

Through her diaries and letters, the reader can see how the war affected daily life, as Virginia describes the effects of the numerous air raids in and around London. For example, towards the end of the war in March 1918, Virginia writes:

> '...the guns went off all round us and we heard the whistles. There was no denying it.'[1]

We get a glimpse into how people at that time coped with the ferocity of the war, by hiding and sleeping in cellars and kitchens. Virginia and Leonard were no different; mattresses were laid down in lower rooms and the time was spent with the servants, Nellie and Lottie. Through this time, Virginia was extremely worried about the safety of her sister Vanessa and her friend, Katherine (Ka) Cox, but everyday life continued despite this – visitors were still received at the house and writing continued. The war was a time of great anxiety for the Woolfs. It would later permeate Virginia's writing, most notably in *Jacob's Room* and *Mrs Dalloway*, started in January 1920 and mid-1922, as *The Hours*, respectively. *Jacob's Room* follows Jacob through his life in Cambridge, London and Greece, places that Virginia had visited. Although not directly referencing the war, the first lines of the novel give a great indication:

> 'So of course," wrote Betty Flanders, pressing her heels rather deeper in the sand, "there was nothing for it but to leave."'.[2]

One of the most well-known poems of the war was written in 1915 by John McCrae, entitled *In Flanders Fields*, and, as some critics have noted, Flanders can be seen as a synonym for death in battle. There is an obvious connection between the character of Jacob and Virginia's deceased brother, Thoby, who died in 1906 aged 25, and it has been suggested that *Jacob's Room* was written not only as an elegy to him, but also to the countless numbers of young men killed in the Great War.

Today, Richmond is fortunate that the buildings at 17 The Green and Hogarth House still stand. They are both Grade II listed as historic buildings, meaning that they are of special interest and every attempt should be made to preserve them. Both properties have recently been renovated. Hogarth House has been graced with a blue plaque that testifies to the years the couple spent there and their creation of The Hogarth Press. Richmond Green remains largely as it was a century ago but Paradise Road is now a busy thoroughfare with regular traffic queues and Hogarth House is surrounded by office buildings and a public car park, but it isn't hard to imagine Virginia watching the army trucks and soldiers on horseback passing along the street a hundred years ago. Being located close to the shops and only five minutes away from the station, the couple were able to easily travel by train to visit friends and family living elsewhere. The house is also close to the River Thames and to the semi-wilderness of the ancient Deer Park at the top of Richmond Hill, which offered the couple many opportunities for delightful walks in the area. Indeed, going for long walks was advised by Virginia's doctors, and Virginia seemed to enjoy walking around the Richmond area, often wandering to Kew Gardens with her dogs, casually observing all manner of life and activity around her.

In her writing, Virginia presents Hogarth House as a solid building, with thick walls and doors, almost like a protective shroud. Leonard also refers to Hogarth House as 'graceful and light', demonstrating that the couple thought of the house not only as a safe haven, but also as a comfortable home. It was, indeed, '...a perfect envelope for everyday life.'[3]

Her first novel, *The Voyage Out*, had received warm reviews, and Virginia was determined to make a name for herself in the literary world. The time she spent living in Hogarth House, could be described as an embryonic period for her development as a novelist, which was to be further enhanced by the creation of the Hogarth Press.

The Hogarth Press

The Hogarth Press began as a hobby for Leonard and

Virginia. In fact, Leonard had decided that it would be useful for Virginia to have something practical to focus on, as her writing and self-absorption took such a toll on her mental health. She needed a distraction from the psychological strain of writing which brought with it the anxiety of never being able to make a name for herself as a respected writer. Having relocated to the suburbs to escape the constant demands of Bloomsbury's hectic social scene, Leonard believed he had found the perfect place for Virginia to recover and settle down to a regular routine. In his autobiography, *Beginning Again*, Leonard describes the moment that the couple saw a printing press in a shop window:

> 'We stared through the window at them rather like two
> hungry children gazing at buns and cakes in a baker
> shop window.'[4]

They attempted to learn the process of printing, but eventually bought a press which came with an instruction manual and they taught themselves from there. Although it was initially a struggle with some setbacks, the couple persisted in their aim to be able to publish their own work and the process of printing and publishing became a source of great joy and pride for both of them.

At the time when their new press was delivered, Virginia was not writing regularly in her diary, but she was sending frequent letters to family and friends. She describes the new arrival with great excitement, but also describes the difficulties with the typesetting process. In a letter to her sister, Vanessa Bell, on April 17th 1917, she says that, '…the arrangement of the type is such a business that we shan't be ready to start printing directly.'[5]

She goes on to describe how the large blocks of type would need to be split into separate letters and fonts, which then have to be placed into the correct partitions.

Unfortunately for Virginia, soon after starting, she confused the h's with the n's, leading them to start the process of typesetting all over again.

In a later letter, she describes Leonard's feeling of never wanting to do anything else but printing and it seems that Virginia is very happy at this particular moment. Their first attempt at producing fiction was in 1917 when they decided to print a short pamphlet which contained two stories; one each by Virginia and Leonard.

Two Stories was officially published in July of the same year and included *Three Jews* by Leonard and *The Mark on the Wall* by Virginia. The pamphlet was around 34 pages long but took the couple more than two months to produce due to the lengthy process of setting the type manually.

The couple had decided that they would publish other authors too, and their second endeavour was *Prelude* by Katherine Mansfield in 1918, followed by Virginia's short story *Kew Gardens* and T.S. Eliot's collected *Poems* in 1919. These first four publications were printed and bound by the Woolfs themselves, but this was not the case for all the publications that followed. In the first four years of the Hogarth Press, the Woolfs had published nine books. It is worth noting the earnings from these books, as laid out in Leonard's autobiography, *Beginning Again*[6]:

Two Stories	£7 1s. 0d.
Prelude	£7 11s. 8d.
Kew Gardens	£14 10s. 0d.
Eliot's *Poems*	£9 6s. 10s.
Murry's *Critic in Judgment*	£2 7s. 0d.
Forster's *Story of the Siren*	£4 3s. 7d.
Mirrlees's *Paris*	£8 2s. 9d.

Stories from the Old Testament	£11 4s.5d.
Gorky's *Reminiscences*	£26 10s. 9d.

With total expenditure amounting to around £38, the total net profit at the end of the first four years was around £90. The couple also paid the author 25 per cent of the gross profits and had to include printing costs when they didn't print and bind the book themselves. What seems incredible, is that even with Virginia's fragile health, leaning on great support from Leonard, they were able to start a small publishing business with no capital. Leonard himself expresses surprise at this fact, and that '…ten years after… the Hogarth Press was a successful commercial publishing business.'

From the publication of *Jacob's Room* in 1922, Virginia decided that she would not write for other publishers again:

> 'A 2nd edition of the *Voyage Out* needed; and another of *Night and Day* shortly; and Nisbet offers me £100 for a book. Oh dear there must be an end of this! Never write for publishers again anyhow.'[8]

Accordingly, all her subsequent work was published by the Hogarth Press. Leonard describes this decision as arising from Virginia's hypersensitivity to criticism, and that publishing her own works without having to suffer the negativity of sending manuscripts to publishers for scrutiny, filled her with delight.[9]

By 1917, the couple were at the centre of a group of emerging writers who wanted to look at the world with fresh eyes. Europe was still in the deadly throes of the Great War which had blighted an entire generation. In Russia, the Tsarist regime had been replaced by a new government, which was overthrown in October by Lenin's Bolsheviks. Leonard Woolf had socialist sympathies and would have understood the importance for workers to control the means of production. He would also likely have known of William Morris' small press, the Kelmscott Press, which published over fifty works in the 1890s, with many books including illustrations by Edward Burne-Jones. This may well have provided a model for their own small press enterprise and their choice to involve Virginia's sister, Vanessa Bell, to design the covers for the books.

This ownership of the means of book production gave both Leonard and Virginia the autonomy to be able to decide their own work schedule; it gave them editorial and artistic freedom too. It could be argued that the facility of the Hogarth Press saved Virginia from further mental instability caused by the demands of outside editors and publishers. As she writes in her diary, before leaving Richmond on January 9th 1924:

> 'Moreover, nowhere else could we have started the Hogarth Press, whose very awkward beginning had rise in this very room, on this very green carpet.'

The slower pace of life in Richmond was clearly beneficial for Virginia too, both for her writing career and her mental health. Apart from the artistic control which the Hogarth Press gave to the couple, it also gave them a measure of financial security too; by April 1938, Virginia writes:

> 'Press worth £10,000 and all this sprung from that type on the drawing room table at Hogarth House 20 years ago.'[10]

Becoming a Writer

Living in Richmond from 1914 to 1924 was a prolific time

for Virginia, the writer. As well as countless essays, reviews and stories, including *Mr Bennett and Mrs Brown*, *Kew Gardens* and *The War from the Street*, she completed and published *Night and Day*, *Monday or Tuesday* and *Jacob's Room*, which, as she mentions in a letter to Philip Morrell in 1938, she describes as her favourite novel. In addition to working on these, during this time period she was also writing *The Common Reader* and *Mrs Dalloway*, which were both published in 1925, a year after leaving Richmond.

In a diary entry in March 1927, Virginia writes; 'So I made up *Jacob's Room* looking at the fire at Hogarth House.' It is no surprise that she was looking at the fire while creating a novel. Virginia's way of writing has been described in great detail by Leonard in his autobiography. Rarely using her writing room to actually write her novels, she would sit in an armchair with a piece of plywood on her knees, upon which she had glued an inkstand[11]. This, according to Leonard, was the way in which she wrote the first drafts of all her novels. While writing, she was completely ensconced in her work, or as Leonard calls it 'writing with concentrated passion'. One can imagine Virginia, sitting by the fire in Hogarth House, furiously working away on one of her novels.

Leonard describes two stages of passion and excitement when Virginia was working on a novel; the first, being the creation or actual writing, during which she would be most concentrated. The second occurred when she was going to send the manuscript to the printers – he called it a 'passion of despair'[12], and it is from this stage that she was most vulnerable to a breakdown. Leonard had witnessed this in 1913 just after she had finished *The Voyage Out*. Again in 1941, Virginia succumbed to this 'passion of despair' after finishing *Between the Acts* and it was this and other factors including the horrors of the Second World War that contributed to her taking her own life a few months later, by drowning in the River Ouse near their Sussex home, Monk's House.

Through her diaries, it is clear that she enjoyed writing *Jacob's Room*, calling it the most amusing novel she had worked on. Aside from the usual falls in confidence, especially with the form of the novel, Virginia found that *Jacob's Room*, although an experiment, left her with an elevated sense of herself, as she writes in her diary: 'There's no doubt in my mind that I have found out how to begin (at 40) to say something in my own voice.'

Jacob's Room was considered to be Woolf's first experimental novel, with critics calling it her first mature work. The narrative is not conventional, but flows from moment to moment, rather like a stream of consciousness. From the diary quote above, it seems that Virginia had finally found the voice that she wanted to present, and this discovery of her writer's voice had its beginnings in Richmond. The writing of *Night and Day*, completed earlier than *Jacob's Room*, seems to have been easier (and certainly was in comparison to the numerous drafts of *The Voyage Out*).

Published in 1919, *Night and Day* follows the romantic lives of two women, Katherine and Mary and reflects the debate about love and marriage that was current at the time. Mary works for a suffrage organisation and although some women had been granted the right to vote in 1918, there was an on-going campaign for all women to be granted suffrage which continued until universal suffrage was finally granted in 1928.

During the First World War, many women left their homes and entered the work place, taking on roles vacated by men who were then on the front line. As the men returned, some women were reluctant to go back to their previous domestic roles. This caused a lively discussion in the press and in society about 'women wanting to wear the trousers'.

Virginia considered *Night and Day* as a development of her work from *The Voyage Out*, as well as having more depth and eschewing a neat resolution. One of her characters, Mary, in *Night and Day*, remains unmarried at the end.

Her novel, *Mrs Dalloway*, emerged from a short story, *Mrs Dalloway in Bond Street*, and was partly written in Richmond where Virginia would have encountered many wounded soldiers recovering from the war. In it, the character of Septimus Smith is suffering from mental frailties and health issues which lead him to jump out of a window to commit suicide; Smith's mental state was as a result of his experiences during the war, and would probably be regarded as PTSD today.

Richmond as a literary setting

Richmond as a literary location, first appears in *The Voyage Out*, written before Virginia moved to Richmond. In the novel, the character of Rachel Vinrace is raised by her two aunts in Richmond, where they like the quiet and Richmond Park. Mrs Hilbery, Katherine's mother in *Night and Day*, also mentions Richmond as part of a day's pleasant outing. Richmond also appears in novels long after Virginia left the town; the stags in the deer park, driving to the town and a marriage proposal are mentioned in *Orlando*, considered Virginia's long love letter to her friend, Vita Sackville-West. Even in *The Years*, the servant Annie Crosby returns to The Green in Richmond with her dog, Rover. The references were not just limited to the novels – in *The Duchess and the Jeweller*, a short story published in *Harper's Bazaar* in 1938, she mentions Oliver Bacon, the rich Jew who had a villa in Richmond overlooking the river. Although these references are short and scant, it demonstrates the influence that

Richmond had on Virginia's imagination.

Henry VII (Earl of Richmond), spent three years constructing Richmond Palace on a grand scale, to rival European palaces of the time. The area around the palace, formerly known as Shene, came to be known as Richmond from around 1500. His son Henry VIII preferred Hampton Court Palace a few miles away and passed Richmond Palace on to his ex-wives. Both of his daughters, Mary and Elizabeth, grew up there and when Elizabeth I became queen, she hosted plays by William Shakespeare in the halls. She died there in 1603.

The Palace was neglected, following Cromwell's Civil War, but royal connections to the town continued, as Richmond Park became a favoured hunting ground of the monarchs of England. Richmond Park is the largest of London's Royal Parks, now a national nature reserve and still home to many wild deer. It has also been designated Grade I status of historic parks and gardens. The Old Deer Park, known as such after 1637, was previously known as The New Park of Richmond, as deemed by Elizabeth I.

The growth of the town increased when the railway was built in 1846 and it became a fashionable place to go for the weekend. Indeed, going to the Star and Garter Hotel on the top of Richmond Hill was one of Charles Dickens' favourite places, where he often went to celebrate family occasions. The hotel was a popular haunt for royalty and wealthy business people too such as the Rothschild family, who owned a house in Gunnersbury nearby. The splendid view westward to Windsor has inspired paintings by both J. M. W. Turner and Sir Joshua Reynolds. It is also described in Sir Walter Scott's novel *The Heart of Midlothian* (1818). Literary residents of the area have included Geoffrey Chaucer, George Eliot, Horace Walpole, Bertrand Russell, Alfred Lord Tennyson and Richard Brinsley Sheridan.

Social Life for the Woolfs

Far from being a recluse, Virginia was a social animal who enjoyed witty conversation and dining with friends. This is clearly demonstrated by the sheer number of visitors the couple received, as well as numerous outings to friends and social gatherings in London. As Leonard writes: 'Virginia loved "Society", its functions and parties, the bigger the better; but she also liked – at any rate in prospect – any party.'[13]

Leonard, on the other hand, did not share the same enjoyment of social events. One of the main reasons for leaving Richmond after ten years was to allow Virginia to enjoy more of a social life in central London. However, even in Richmond, with its journey by train from Waterloo, the couple had many visitors; 'On the whole, L and I are becoming celebrities.'[14] While this was extremely pleasing for Virginia, for Leonard this was not the case. She thrived on meeting people, having in-depth conversations and the excitement of gatherings. Although, as Leonard writes, Virginia was aware of the mental strain of her social life and the need to protect herself from too much nervous agitation. In addition to individual parties, Virginia and Leonard belonged to various clubs and societies, such as The 1917 Club, and The Memoir Club. The 1917 Club, partly founded by Leonard, brought together artists and politicians of similar intellect and ideas. This was a place where Virginia would meet many of her contemporaries; this is frequently mentioned in the first two editions of her diaries.

The Memoir Club was set up by Molly MacCarthy in the 1920s and continued in various forms until the 1960s. This was a place where the members would read autobiographical papers. However, the group that Virginia is most associated with is the Bloomsbury Group. Otherwise called the Bloomsbury Set, which comprised ten core members, including Virginia and Leonard. The remaining eight were Vanessa and Clive Bell, E.M. Forster, Roger Fry, Duncan Grant, John Maynard Keynes, Desmond MacCarthy and Lytton Strachey. Named after the area of London where many of its members lived, the Bloomsbury Group was essentially a group of friends, which grew out of meetings at Cambridge University. As Leonard noted, the idea of this group has been perpetuated by the 'outside world'— he regarded it as a myth which did not really exist. It is possible that Bloomsbury came to signify a cultural attitude towards life and society, but the notion of Bloomsbury will forever be associated with Virginia.

What follows is an analysis of the time Virginia spent in Richmond — her thoughts, daily life, work and rest — as revealed by her diaries and letters, to explore how living in the town influenced her life and development as a writer. The quotes garnered from her personal work demonstrate her true feelings about Richmond, which have unfortunately been tainted by the false quote in the film *The Hours*, directed by Stephen Daldry with a screenplay by Sir David Hare. The fictitious quote is said by the actress Nicole Kidman, playing Virginia Woolf, at a train station and is as follows; 'If it is a choice between Richmond and death, I choose death.' The screenplay is based on Michael Cunningham's book *The Hours*, and the editor can reveal that the majority of the station scene in the film was largely invented by Sir David Hare.

Virginia's Richmond

London is incredibly beautiful – not with the soft suburban beauty of Richmond.

– Letter to Katherine Arnold-Foster, 12 April 1924

After Virginia's mental collapse in 1913, in which she took an overdose of veronal, Leonard had to decide whether to have his wife certified as insane and admitted to an asylum. To avoid this, doctors agreed that if Virginia could be cared for by her husband and nurses, then she need not be certified. The couple's rooms at 13 Clifford's Inn were not suitable for this, so George Duckworth, who was Virginia's half-brother, allowed the couple to stay at his house in Sussex. After a short period of time, it was agreed that Virginia could be moved, and thus, they went to live at Asheham House, the Woolfs' country home near Rodmell, in East Sussex and stayed there until 1914. While staying there, Virginia seemed to recover slightly and was taken on a couple of short holidays to places such as Cornwall, Northumberland and Somerset. Considered successful, the couple decided to look for a home closer to London; close enough for Leonard's political activity, but far enough away to reduce the opportunity for impromptu social visits.

Virginia and Leonard Woolf moved to Richmond in southwest London in mid-October 1914, after several weeks of house-hunting. While renting rooms at 17 The Green, Richmond, they sent for their furniture and belongings which had been in storage since moving out of 13 Clifford's Inn, where they had been living from 1912 for a year. The rooms they let were overlooking a large park and near to the station, the shops, Richmond Theatre and the library. It seemed to be a good base for the couple to look for a permanent home. Leonard described Mrs le Grys, their Belgian landlady, as an 'extremely nice, plump, excitable flibberti-gibbet, about 35 to 40 years old'[1]. Virginia echoes this impression of their landlady:

> '…my conviction that Mrs le Grys is the best tempered woman in England, and if she gets her 20 roomed house at Southampton, will make it a gigantic success.'[2]

Mrs le Grys was aided in the house by her servant, Lizzy, who, according to Leonard, was not entirely an asset to the household; Virginia notes an incident on January 11th 1915, in which a fire breaks out in one of the rented rooms where Lizzy had been attempting to light the fire, but instead had set light to curtains spreading to a Japanese screen. Lizzy is further admonished by Virginia when she complains that Lizzy had '…smashed two very nice bits of china for us.'[3] Lizzy's unfortunate clumsiness continues just a few days later on January 14th when Virginia reports another 'mere' fire in the kitchen. Virginia's sense of humour in regard to the situation is evident later in the diary entry when she writes that they, '…must give [Lizzy] something cheap to break her rage against.'[4]

Virginia had restarted her diary at the beginning of the year, and goes into detail about everyday life at The Green. She describes sitting down to breakfast with Mrs le Grys, who complains about the refugees from the war living in her house and their eating habits. She also records the couple's writing habits, with Leonard writing reviews and

Virginia continuing work on '...poor Effie's story'[5], which is unidentified and has since disappeared. During this writing period at The Green, Virginia reflected upon her craft in a diary entry on January 6th 1915:

> 'I wrote all the morning with infinite pleasure, which is queer, because I know all the time that there is no reason to be pleased with what I write, and that in 6 weeks or even days, I shall hate it.'[6]

It might be that she was working on the revisions of *The Voyage Out*, which she had begun in 1910, but was still working on the manuscript; it wasn't published until March 1915. However, in her diary she mentions *The Third Generation*, which might have been a new work or connected to Effie's story, but this has been lost or was never finished. Even with the difficulty with *The Voyage Out*, Virginia writes:

> 'I thought how happy I was, without any of the excitements which, once, seemed to me to constitute happiness.'

Diaries, 16 January 1915

It is entirely possible that Virginia is referring to the 'excitements' of central London, with the distractions of the area. It is interesting to note that in the same diary entry she writes; 'My writing now delights me solely because I love writing.' It was clear that the contrast of Richmond to central London was beginning to have a positive effect.

While looking for a home in Richmond, the Woolfs discovered Hogarth House on Paradise Road nearby, and immediately were taken with the property. However, there were difficulties and delays with the lease and so they continued to search for a permanent home. In the following extracts, Virginia expresses her deep desire at acquiring Hogarth House and the excitement she feels upon finally getting the lease; the quote from her letter to Margaret Llewelyn Davies is a perfect example of how Virginia felt about the house:

> 'We walked to Hogarth this afternoon, to see if the noise of school-children is really a drawback. Apparently, it would only affect Suffield. Well – I wonder what we shall do. I'd give a lot to turn over 30 pages or so, and find written down what happens to us.'

Diaries, 15 January 1915

It seems that Virginia was excited about the possibility of moving into Hogarth House, so much so that she longs to look into the future to see what happens. Ten days later, at tea with Leonard, some decisions are made:

> 'At tea we decided three things: in the first place to take Hogarth, if we can get it; in the second, to buy a Printing press; in the third to buy a Bull dog, probably called John. I am very much excited at the idea of all three.'

Diaries, 25 January 1915

It appears that the 'tea meeting' decisions mostly came true, with the exception of a bulldog called John. In addition to the charms of Hogarth House, Virginia also seemed to enjoy the environment in Richmond, calling it '…the first of the suburbs by a long way, because it is not an offshoot of London, any more than Oxford or Marlborough is.'[7] Virginia often described her pleasure at searching for houses, but Hogarth House seemed to be superior to the rest:

> 'I have a nose for a house, and that was a perfect house, if ever there was one.'

Diaries, 30 January 1915

Already living in Richmond, at 17 The Green, Virginia and Leonard could walk around the town and return via Paradise Road to look at Hogarth House, surely dreaming of the time they could call it their own:

'…we walked after lunch in the Park, and came home by way of Hogarth, and tried to say that we shan't be much disappointed if we don't get it.'

Diaries, 31 January 1915

Just a day later, their Belgian landlady, Mrs le Grys, told Virginia about another house available on The Green, but it did not have the charms as Hogarth House. Although the signing of the lease was still a couple of weeks in the future, Virginia was certain what that future would hold:

'In fact, it seems quite likely at this moment that we shall get Hogarth. I wish it were tomorrow. I am certain it is the best house to take.'

Diaries, 1 February 1915

Even before the lease was signed, Virginia was writing about 'their' house to her friends:

'I do hope you'll come and see us often in our house – Hogarth House – It's far the nicest house in England.'

Letter to Margaret Llewelyn Davies, 22 February 1915

The lure of the house didn't leave them, and in late February or early March 1915, Leonard acquired the lease for Hogarth, but suddenly, Virginia's health deteriorated rapidly, and Leonard was forced to acquire nurses to look after her. In *Beginning Again*, Leonard describes his desire not to allow Mrs le Grys' house to be turned into a mental hospital, and therefore he arranged for Hogarth House to be prepared immediately for the couple to move into, along with four nurses. Leonard describes the first few weeks in Hogarth House as terrifying, and after some time, Virginia deteriorated so badly that she fell into a coma. Thankfully, by the end of 1915, Virginia had recovered well enough to do without nurses.

In *Downhill All the Way*, Leonard goes into much detail about the origins of Hogarth House; stating that it was thought to have been originally built in 1720 for Lord Suffield and was converted into two properties in the nineteenth century. However, he goes on to expose this claim as false, by stating that the barony of Suffield was not created until much later in the 1700s, therefore meaning that the information on the house was false, and thus, the origin of the house was still unknown. The manner in which he describes the house is one of admiration, commenting on the grandeur of the rooms, and it is clear that he enjoyed living there. However, towards the end of 1919, the couple were given some bad news from their landlady at Hogarth House:

> 'Mrs Brewer has told us that she means to sell Hogarth and Suffield, and we are considering buying them both – together with a greater number than usual of diners, letters, telephone calls, books to review, reviews of my book, invitations to parties and so forth.'

Diaries, 28 November 1919

This presented an opportunity to buy the property. They bought both the adjoining house Suffield House and Hogarth House for between £1950 and £2000, according to different sources:

> 'We've gone and bought Hogarth and the house next door.'

Letter to Katherine Arnold-Foster, 1 January 1920

Hogarth House remained their home until they moved to Tavistock Square in March 1924. By June 1923, Virginia had become a well-known writer, with many invitations to give talks and attend gatherings. She confided to her diary that the couple must move into central London, but that Leonard had yet to be convinced. He was most likely worried that the stress both of the move and the added demands on her time would be harmful to her health.

At this point in her literary career, Virginia was writing *Mrs Dalloway*, originally entitled *The Hours*, where one of the themes is the passing of time. The plot encompasses one day, and through this day, the characters notice the loss of time, often by the striking of Big Ben. With this ingenious plot device, it is possible that Woolf is emphasizing the importance of small decisions that might affect one's life, endlessly marching towards its end.

In her diary, Virginia expresses horror at the impending move, but closes with 'Still this is life – never to be sitting down for longer than one feels inclined.'[8] For Virginia, it was clear that she missed the excitement of central London, but for Leonard, it was an entirely different matter; '...the house would have been much too large for us and we had decided that it was time to move back into London.'[9] After buying both Hogarth and Suffield, the couple had toyed with the idea of reuniting the two halves of the building to make it a large home to live in for the rest of their lives. It appeared that Richmond had done its job for Virginia: it had helped her regain her health. Leonard describes the years at Hogarth as:

> '...crucial for the stabilizing of her mind and health and for her work...I am sure that this tranquil atmosphere helped to tranquilize her mind.'

Downhill All the Way:16

Virginia was well aware that the change of living arrangements would be a momentous one. She appeared to be thankful that the couple had no children to think about, but still classified her 'family' as including her two servants:

> 'It's odd how entirely this house question absorbs one. It is a radical change, though. It means a revision of 4 lives…We have no children to consider. My health is as good as it will be in this world, and a great deal better than it ever has been.'[10]

The next few months were concerned with finding a new home in central London, and Virginia records several visits to view numerous houses. On January 9th 1924, Virginia writes in her diary that they had secured a ten-year lease on 52 Tavistock Square. It is at this moment that readers of Virginia's diary fully realise how connected she felt with Richmond, even though she was leaving it behind:

> 'So I ought to be grateful to Richmond and Hogarth, and indeed, whether it's my invincible optimism or not, I am grateful. Nothing could have suited better all through those years when I was creeping about, like a rat struck on the head, and the aeroplanes were over London at night, and the streets dark, and no penny buns in the window. Moreover, nowhere else could we have started the Hogarth Press, whose very awkward beginning had rise in this very room, on this very green carpet. Here that strange offspring grew and throve; it ousted us from the dining room, which is now a dusty coffin; and crept all over the house.
>
> And people have been here, thousands of them it seems to me. I've sat over this fire many an evening talking, and save for one fit of the glooms last summer, have never complained of Richmond, till I shed it, like a loose skin.

I've had some very curious visions in this room too,
lying in bed, mad, and seeing the sunlight quivering
like gold water, on the wall. I've heard the voices of the
dead here. And felt, through it all, exquisitely happy.'

Diaries, 9 January 1924

In this extremely important and expressive diary entry,
Virginia pays tribute to Hogarth House and the area of
Richmond. It is possible that the couple could not have
founded the Hogarth Press in any other place; it certainly
would have had a different name. In fact, five years earlier,
Virginia had written:

'I see us settled for life, with Hogarth, Monk's House,
and two domestics.'[11]

Time, however, moves on and the needs of people
change. On March 12th 1924, Virginia wrote her last ever
entry at Hogarth House, beginning:

'And I'm now going to write the very last pages ever
to be written at Hogarth House. First; the state of the
weather. It's as if a fine veil had descended and lay,
clear, over the chimneys; which are a pale yellow, and
brick red.'[12]

The most telling extract from this diary entry is the
moment when Virginia gives her final thanks to Hogarth:

'Nor at the moment can I think of any farewell for this
beautiful and lovable house, which has done us such a
good turn for almost precisely nine years, so that, as I
lay in bed last night, I nearly humanised it, and offered
it my thanks.'

Diaries, 12 March 1924

Virginia would often compare Richmond favourably to central London:

> 'Richmond is certainly the place to live in, partly because then London becomes so full of romance.'

Letter to Duncan Grant, 15 November 1915

By 1916, Virginia already thinks of the River Thames at Richmond as her river. In this wonderful quotation from a letter to Margaret Llewelyn Davies, Virginia writes:

> 'Do you ever get out onto your Heath? I often think of you, as I pace beside my river, which surely surpasses anything you have.'

Letter to Margaret Llewelyn Davies, 23 January 1916

Although Richmond was her home, Virginia still liked to visit central London, sometimes to meet friends or see relatives, but sometimes just to soak up the atmosphere. However, she admits that she likes getting back to Richmond:

> 'London goes on much as usual. I dip in occasionally, and shake my ears well when I get back to the purer air of Richmond…I do think Richmond has great charms also, and now we have Roger's servants, we keep clean.'

Letter to Katherine Cox, 12 February 1916

In a very revealing letter to her sister, Virginia confirms that she is seduced by the charms of central London, but is thankful that she doesn't live there, instead, preferring the simplicities and refined nature of Richmond, as she expressed in her letter to Violet Dickinson, four years later:

> London always seems to me rich in romance when I dip into it, which I do about twice a week, but thank

God I don't live there.'

Letter to Vanessa Bell, 11 February 1917

'I think it would be very good for your morals to visit the simplicities and refinements of Richmond.'

Letter to Violet Dickinson, 5 February 1921

It seems apparent that Virginia enjoyed living in Richmond, as she even advocated it to her friend Ottoline Morrell as preferable to London:

'Shan't you ever come to London – or rather, since London is useless, to Richmond?'

Letter to Lady Ottoline Morrell, 8 November 1921

As the years in Richmond continued, Virginia comments on everyday life, often including observations on the weather and their garden. As with a lot of her diary entries, it could be argued that Virginia used daily writing as an opportunity to practise her craft of writing, and this can be seen with the following quotes, specifically chosen for their linguistic beauty:

'I'm sitting wedged in the window, and so catch almost on my head the steady drip of rain which is pattering on the leaves.'

Diaries, 19 July 1919

'Here I sit at Richmond, and like a lantern stood in the middle of a field my light goes up in darkness. Melancholy diminishes as I write. Why then don't I write it down oftener?'

Diaries, 25 October 1920

Although she might be feeling melancholy, Virginia sees

herself here as the light in the darkness. This could be symbolic of her recovery from her mental illnesses that had plagued her over the previous years. Yet it seems that writing her diary helped her feel stronger and provided some kind of therapeutic outlet:

> 'We dine over the fire. L has his tray on a little stool. We are as comfortable as cottagers (looked at through the window)'

> Diaries, 14 February 1922

> 'We walked out in our mackintoshes, up the river and down the Avenue. Scarcely a couple to be seen. I pitied the orange barrows, half covered over, with some wet man sheltering near under a tree, his Sunday sales demolished.'

> Diaries, 5 May 1918

Virginia also wrote about their new business venture the Hogarth Press. Here, she mentions McDermott, the printer in Richmond. He became friendly with the couple and even helped with some of their printing for the Hogarth Press, although not altogether successful:

> 'The only small printer we know is McDermott, Duke Street, Richmond. I think he would probably do your catalogue in time, and much cheaper than you could get in London. You would have to instruct him rather carefully about type and so on.'

> Letter to Vanessa Bell, 27 March 1921

Later in 1921, the couple were doing more and more printing, and therefore decided to buy another printing press to put in the basement of Hogarth House:

> 'We have just bought a press for £70 and are turning

the basement into a printing shop. Ralph comes every day. I walk through the woods of Richmond which are yellow, but the weather is like in early May, and think of you; oh and other things.'

Letter to Vanessa Bell, 24 October 1921

She often wrote about the life she saw while walking around Richmond, which she was recommended to do by her doctors. As the final quotes in this section show, Woolf had a fondness for the local area:

'We shall count upon your coming here. I think I shall invite a small, and select party to meet you – or would you like a drunken riot? I want to give a party. We might take a float upon the river.'

Letter to Vanessa Bell, 26 April 1917

Richmond Park was a source of great pleasure for Virginia, and in addition she could also walk by the river, which she had already claimed as her own:

'We took a walk in the old style through the Park, down the avenue and back by the river, which was flooding up fast, and cut us off, making us creep along a railing so as to reach dry land. The streets remind me of Cambridge streets. People walk down the middle.'

Diaries, 15 December 1917

Setting up the Hogarth Press was a demanding project too, which she enjoyed in partnership with Leonard:

'I can't say much for the beauty of Richmond at this moment. We're so busy printing that we hardly notice… Well, I must immediately wash, for I'm all over printers ink, and the Mothers arrive in 20 minutes.'

Letter to Nicholas Bagenal, 15 April 1918

'We think we now deserve some good luck. Yet I daresay we're the happiest couple in England.'

Diaries, 28 December 1919

Virginia continued her excursions into central London to places like Gordon Square, where she had once lived, but she didn't regret leaving Bloomsbury as there was a sense of not being constantly on show in Richmond:

'I like coming back to Richmond after Gordon S[quare]. I like continuing our private life, unseen by anyone.'

Diaries, 11 May 1920

Her work for the Hogarth Press provided her with a sense of purpose and achievement, and brought her into contact with other writers and new ideas:

'I ought to say how happy I am, since one of these pages said how unhappy I was. I can't see any reason in it. My only guess is that it has something to do with working steadily; writing things out of my head; and never having a compartment empty.'

Diaries, 19 December 1920

'Anyhow, I am content at present, or moderately so. I am alive; rather energetic.'

Diaries, 8 July 1923

Virginia seemed to be growing and developing, happy to be working with her husband Leonard as a small publisher, earning her own money as a writer from writing reviews and essays. She was soaking up the environment, and the natural beauty of the area no doubt lifted her spirits. Each day, she was storing up her observations to be incorporated in her later writing. She often mentioned the qualities of nature that she viewed, quite possibly walking with her dogs:

> '...then we take Max for a walk. Halfway up to the Bridge, we found ourselves cut off by the river, which rose visibly, with little ebb and flow, like the pulse of a heart... '

Diaries, 2 January 1915

One of her favourite places to walk in Richmond was the Old Deer Park, although this was probably surpassed by walks along the River Thames:

> 'After lunch we took the air in the Old Deer Park and marked by a line of straw how high the river had been; and how a great tree had fallen across the towing path, crushing the railing beneath it.'

Diaries, 5 January 1915

Virginia became adept at recording details in her diaries, honing her skills as a writer by doing so. In one diary extract, on January 9th 1915, she notices that Richmond Bridge had been damaged while she was out walking to Kingston. It transpired that a few barges had broken loose from their moorings on the river, and crashed into the bridge 'knocking a good deal of stone from one of the arches.'[13] She notes in the same entry that they 'had a good walk.' She also records moments of everyday, mundane life in Richmond:

> 'I pottered about buying small fragments of meat and vegetables and got some books out of the Library. I believe we shall find it more useful than the London Library, as no one, save ourselves, reads solid books.'

Diaries, 12 January 1915

In one of her more amusing diary entries, Virginia

describes a walk with Max, her dog, who unfortunately gets injured. Later in the quotation, she talks of being happy without the excitements of her previous life.

> 'I took Max along the River, but we were a good deal impeded, by a bone he stole, by my suspenders coming down, by a dogfight in which his ear was torn and bled horribly. I thought how happy I was, without any of the excitements which, once, seemed to me to constitute happiness.'

Diaries, 16 January 1915

Even when the weather was not very attractive, Virginia would walk around the Richmond area and still find beauty:

> 'Outside it is very cold and grey too. We walked in Richmond Park this afternoon; the trees all black, and the sky heavy over London; but there is enough colour to make it even lovelier today than on bright days, I think. The deer exactly match the bracken.'

Diaries, 19 January 1915

An interesting entry, dated February 1917, demonstrates that Virginia liked to use all of the facilities that Richmond and the Park had to offer. The Pen Ponds, which were created in the 1700s, is a lake divided by a causeway. In 1917, the ponds must have frozen over:

> 'We are going skating today on the Pen Ponds and tomorrow we have induced Lytton to come too.'

Letter to Saxon Sydney Turner, 3 February 1917

Once more, mundane tasks are written into Virginia's diary, but this entry is for preparing for the bombing raids:

> 'I made two little excursions into Richmond, one to discover the right way of spelling Mynah; the other

to buy a new battery, price 1/3…I think it's wise to have mine in readiness for the raid, though three tradespeople of Richmond know for certain that there will never be another.'

Diaries, 23 January 1918

Dogs had always played an important part in Virginia's life as objects of affection. When she was young, the family had a terrier called Shag, but not long after her father's death, Shag was struck by a hansom cab. She was so fond of Shag, Virginia wrote an obituary for him and sent it to *The Guardian*. Soon after her mother's death, the family acquired a new puppy called Jerry, but the fate of Jerry is not revealed by the diaries. Gurth, a sheep-dog puppy soon followed and was taken to live with Vanessa after her marriage. Adrian, Virginia's younger brother, and Vanessa decided that they wanted another dog, and went to Battersea Dogs Home and came back with Hans, a Boxer.

As has been seen in previous quotes, Virginia goes walking in Richmond with a new dog, Max, but soon after the appearance of Tinker, Max disappears from the diary. Tinker came into Virginia's life when a neighbour asked the couple to look after the Clumber spaniel while he was away in the war. Tinker must have had a big impact on Virginia as she laments the outcome of the dog's story.

'The chief fact today I think is the development and discovery of Tinker's character – all in the right direction. He was taken on a long walk by the river the avenue and the Park; his spirit is great, but almost under control. He fell into the river twice; jumped out again.'

Diaries, 15 October 1917

VIRGINIA WOOLF IN RICHMOND

We are faced with the problem of providing for Tinker. His spirits make him an exacting guest. We went to find a home with the Vet. today, and discovered that a Vet. lives in part of the great red house at the back of us.'

Diaries, 26 October 1917

'The melancholy fact is that Tinker, at the present moment, 5.30, is lost…This was discovered at lunch time. When we had done, L went off to look in the neighbourhood, but without success…However, we were rather dashed by the loss of the spaniel whom we had come to like.'

Diaries, 6 November 1917

In later life, Virginia had another dog called Pinka and she was so fond of dogs that she even wrote a story from the perspective of the poet Elizabeth Barrett Browning's dog, called *Flush*, which was published in 1933.

The river at Richmond features a great deal in her diaries too, with Virginia once calling it 'her river'. The changing nature of the river clearly interested her, and a lot of her fiction had clear connections to water; one very obvious example being her experimental novel *The Waves*. The way she describes seasonal changes in the local landscape is perfectly captured in the following quotes:

'We walked on the river bank in a cold wind, under a grey sky. Both agreed that life seen without illusion is a ghastly affair. Illusions wouldn't come back. However, they returned about 8.30, in front of the fire, and were going merrily until bedtime, when some antics ended the day.'

Diaries, 10 November 1917

'A very cold day. Indeed, I might have remarked the beginning of winter. No leaves to speak of left on the trees now; a sharp chill in the air. One's room after tea most emphatically a little centre of light in the midst of profound darkness.'

Diaries, 13 November 1917

Once again, Virginia talks about being a light in the middle of darkness. This could be taken to be the darkness of the Great War which seemed never to be coming to an end, or could equally allude to keeping her depression at bay, and her room, a room of her own, was the light. Hogarth House was proving to be her sanctuary:

'We … reach the river and see everything reflected perfectly straightly in the water. The red roof of a house had its own little cloud of red in the river – lights lit on the bridge made long streaks of yellow – very peaceful, and as if the heart of winter.'

Diaries, 22 November 1917

On one occasion, while the couple were walking by the river, they saw a tree which was burning. Virginia describes the event in great detail, writing that a crowd had gathered and one man told them that the fire was to get rid of an old tree, whereas another man wasn't too sure. Nevertheless, the couple reported the incident to the police station:

'We walked along the river in the afternoon, when L. came back from Staines, and came to an old hollow elm tree, in the sawdust of which someone so we guessed, had struck a match. The wind was blowing in, and soon the flames were running high…Meanwhile the tree burnt rather beautifully.'

Diaries, 3 December 1917

VIRGINIA WOOLF IN RICHMOND

Passing over Richmond Bridge, it is a short walk along the river to Marble Hill Park in Twickenham. The large park consists of the former grounds of Marble Hill House, now owned by English Heritage: it comprises a Palladian Villa set on the riverside and once home to Henrietta Howard, the mistress of George II. Describing the area as heavenly, Virginia is buoyed up by the mild weather and local life:

> 'I went along the river to Marble Hill. I must retract what I said about the Hell of the year. We have glimpses of Heaven. So mild that the landing window is open, and I sat by the river watching a boat launched, and half expected to see buds on the willows.'

Diaries, 23 January 1918

Virginia often had a sense of duality – of opposites – in her writing. She could also be drawn to dark and grisly happenings. In 1903, a young doctor called Sophia Frances Hickman went missing and her body was found in the woods in Richmond Park. At the inquest, it was found that Miss Hickman had committed suicide by morphia poisoning, and the woods where she was found would subsequently prove a popular suicide spot. Virginia was obviously aware of the story, and during the war, she visited the place with Desmond MacCarthy:

> 'I wandered through Richmond Park in the moonlight with Desmond. We jumped a palisade into Miss Hickman's funeral grove, and found the dark green mounds pointed with red rosettes. The rhododendron is a lovely flower for the moonlight. And we beheld a china watercloset also lovely in the moonlight, the divinity of a sheltered lodger, wedged in among the ferns and the flowering bushes.'

Diaries, 28 May 1918

Virginia describes Richmond on a Saturday as being like a lime tree in bloom; presumably with many people in the streets, rushing about on their business. However, Virginia seems to identify herself as a serene onlooker:

> 'Accurately described, today is a fine spring day, not a hot summer one – so L. and I shaded it off, walking up to the Park this afternoon. But Richmond on fine Saturdays is like a lime tree in full flower suppose one were an insect sitting on the flower. All the others swarm and buzz, and burble. Being residents, we don't, of course.'

Diaries, 15 May 1920

Virginia became part of the local community, by joining the Women's Co-operative Guild, and for four years she was involved in arranging speakers for the Richmond branch to be held at Hogarth House.

Her friend, Margaret Llewelyn Davies, to whom Virginia wrote many letters, was general secretary of the Guild from 1889 to 1921 and by 1910, she had increased the membership of the Guild to 32,000 members. The dedication that Virginia showed to the Guild is evidence of her strong affiliation with the area, such as the attempt to set up a bread shop as well as trying to help educate local women. Virginia often talked about the Guild in her letters, including some of the events and talks that took place:

> 'We had a very remarkable Guild meeting last night, which I must tell you about. A speaker from the Civil Liberty Council, lectured us upon Venereal Diseases, and moral risks for our sons. I felt that the audience was queer, and as no one spoke, I got up and thanked her.'

Letter to Margaret Lleywelyn Davies, 24 January 1917

The above-mentioned meeting caused quite a stir, and led to a couple of the ladies walking out. Upon hearing from Nellie, her servant, about the reasons for the walk out, Virginia and Nellie sat down to discuss the topic of sexual health which shows that they had a close and fairly open relationship. Virginia was not just concerned with the sexual health of her community, but also about the problems of providing food for those who were going hungry due to the war:

> 'Two meetings of the Guild I've presided over. We are trying to set up a Bread Shop here...Mrs Langston is helping the ladies of Richmond to found a Communal Kitchen...Anyhow, according to Mrs Langston they're going to make a mess of it. I propose to get our food there.'

Letter to Margaret Llewelyn Davies, 2 May 1917

There is no evidence to suggest that a bread shop was opened, or a communal kitchen appeared, but the fact that Virginia wanted to support these shows an affection for the people of the area in which she lived. She also helped to organise other talks for the Guild:

> 'Now I have to go with Miss Fry to lecture the Women of Richmond upon prison reform - According to her - if this cheers you at all the criminals are the good people invariably.'

Letter to Lady Robert Cecil, 9 May 1921

Miss Fry was Margery Fry, Roger Fry's sister, and she worked for the Howard League for Penal Reform. This was a charity which campaigned for, and still campaigns for, safer communities and fewer inmates in prison. However, Virginia was rather mocking of the time her brother Adrian was invited to speak at the Guild:

> 'That is my terrible destiny in 30 minutes. Adrian, my
> brother, is coming to speak to the 12 Co-operators of
> Richmond, good working women who mind the pot
> and smack the baby, upon the possibilities of psycho-
> analysis.'

Letter to Will Arnold Forster, 7 November 1922

In the decade that she spent in Richmond, Virginia's diaries reveal that she led a busy life as a writer, small business owner, wife, animal lover, and member of the local Co-op. The natural beauty of her surroundings lifted her spirits, giving her the energy to work on her writing. Her long, meditative walks around the area provided the time and mental space for creative thought. Her regular letter writing and diary entries helped her hone her skills to express her sharp observations and develop her original voice.

As a couple who worked together and enjoyed socialising with the same group of friends, both Leonard and Virginia seemed to have a real fondness for Richmond, and in particular they loved Hogarth House with its elegant rooms and large windows. They created a comfortable home there, as well as making good use of the basement for their growing publishing business.

The Hogarth Press

Have you heard about our Printing Press? We're both so excited that we can talk and think of nothing else.

Letter to Margaret Llewelyn Davies, 22 February 1915

Virginia and Leonard first talked of taking up printing in 1915. Virginia records in her diary on her birthday, January 25th 1915, the three things that had been decided at tea; to buy Hogarth House, to buy a printing press and to get a bulldog called John. Virginia wrote about her excitement about the press to her friend, Margaret Llewelyn Davies in the quote above. In the same letter, she writes:

> 'I think there's a chance of damaging the Webb influence irretrievably (which is my ambition in life). Presses only cost £17.17, and can be worked easily.'

Letter to Margaret Llewelyn Davies, 22 February 1915

It is entirely possible that 'the Webb influence' refers to Beatrice and Sidney Webb, who were at the core of the Fabian Society, a socialist organisation. Leonard had been noticed by the Webbs and had written a couple of articles on socialism and eventually joined the Fabian Society in 1916. Virginia's interest in politics was certainly not as strong as Leonard's:

> 'Virginia was the least political animal that has lived since Aristotle invented the definition.'[1]

Although Virginia might have seen the Hogarth Press as a way to keep Leonard away from the Socialist Webbs, Leonard saw the Press as a way to keep Virginia busy and take her mind off her writing, the strain of which had led to her becoming ill in the past.

Later in 1915, Virginia fell into another depression, and she was eventually moved into Hogarth House with four nurses to attend her. This setback forced the idea of a printing press into the background. However, the idea resurfaced in 1916, with their press being delivered in April 1917:

'I hope we shall get the press this summer and start in the autumn. The question now is, who will write for us? Will you? We shall certainly want some endpapers.

Letter to Vanessa Bell, 28 June 1916

'Our press arrived on Tuesday. We unpacked it with enormous excitement, finally with Nelly's help, carried it into the drawing room, set it on its stand – and discovered it was smashed in half! It is a great weight, and they never screwed it down; but the shop has probably got a spare part. Anyhow the arrangement of the type is such a business that we shan't be ready to start printing directly. One has great blocks of type, which have to be divided into their separate letters, and founts, and then put in the right partitions. The work of ages, especially when you mix the h's with the ns, as I did yesterday... I see that real printing will devour one's entire life.'

Letter to Vanessa Bell, 26 April 1917

It is interesting to note that Leonard does not mention that the press was damaged in any way. Neither Virginia nor Leonard had had any printing experience. Although Virginia had shown an interest in book-binding previously, Leonard describes that they went to St. Bride's school of printing near Fleet Street, but they discovered that only trade union apprentices could learn the process of printing there: 'This seemed to end our career as printers before it could begin.'[2] However, they passed a printing shop near Holborn called Excelsior Printing Supply Co. and explained their problem to one of the workers. Not only did they purchase a printer, small enough to place on the kitchen table, but they also bought a pamphlet which would teach them how to use it.

> '...following the directions in the pamphlet we found that we could pretty soon set the type, lock it up in the chase, ink the rollers, and machine a fairly legible printed page.'

Beginning Again[3]

Their first trial was a pamphlet, mostly for their friends, advertising their first publication. After about a month of practice, the couple decided to print their first publication, which was to be a short 32-page pamphlet containing two stories, which incorporated *The Mark on the Wall* by Virginia and *Three Jews* by Leonard. They printed around 150 copies and bound each copy themselves. Learning the process of printing was not easy, but the couple found it extremely enjoyable:

> 'After 2 hours work at the press, Leonard heaved a terrific sigh and said I wish to God we'd never bought the cursed thing! To my relief, though not surprise, he added Because I shall never do anything else. You can't think how exciting, soothing, ennobling and satisfying it is. '

Letter to Margaret Llewelyn Davies, 2 May 1917

Indeed, it soon became clear that printing was going to become a huge part of their lives, taking precedence over many other things which had previously been seen as important:

> 'We've been so absorbed in printing that I am about as much of a farmyard sheep dog as you are. I can hardly tear myself away to go to London or see anyone.

Letter to Vanessa Bell, 22 May 1917

The main idea for the press, as previously mentioned, was to give Virginia a distraction from her own work to prevent her from becoming sick again, but Leonard also believed that the Hogarth Press would publish work '…which would have little or no chance of being published by ordinary publishers.'[4] One thing that set the Press apart from other publishers was the binding paper and woodcuts that the couple chose to use. They decided to bind each copy using '…beautiful, uncommon and sometimes cheerful paper for binding our books.'[5]

> 'I have heard of a shop where you can get wonderful coloured papers. We're half way through L's story – it gets ever so much quicker, and the fascination is something extreme.'

Letter to Vanessa Bell, 8 June 1917

The publication of *Two Stories* was thought to be a success, having sold 134 copies in total, and this comes from a couple who had never printed before and learned the art of printing from an instruction manual. It seems that Virginia was already thinking along the lines of becoming more professional:

> 'We have just got a handsome sum back on our income tax, which we mean to spend on a press (I need hardly

say) which will print 8 pages at a time, and then we shall be very professional.'

Letter to Vanessa Bell, 27 June 1917

In a letter to Violet Dickinson, Virginia thanks her for liking *Two Stories* and outlines the couple's plans for the future:

> 'We are very glad you like the book. It is tremendous fun doing it, and we are now in treaty for a much larger press and mean to take it up seriously and produce novels with it. And we are even getting an apprentice!'

Letter to Violet Dickinson, 21 July 1917

The couple enlisted help with the Press from various relatives and friends over the years. One of the first to help them with some printing equipment was Emma 'Toad' Vaughan. Emma, Virginia's cousin on her mother's side (daughter of Julia's sister Adeline), seemed to feature more heavily in Virginia's early life, as mentioned in *A Passionate Apprentice*, the volume containing Virginia's early journals:

> We took a proof of the first page of K.M's [Katherine Mansfield's] story, *The Prelude*. It looks very nice, set solid in the new type. Masses of bookbinding equipment from Emma Vaughan arrived this morning – rather a testimony to her fads, for it is all good, and I suppose she never bound a book.

Diaries, 9 October 1917

Alix Sargant-Florence was first introduced to Virginia by Lytton Strachey's younger brother, James. James would marry Alix later, in 1920, but in 1917, Alix expressed an interest in working with the Hogarth Press:

> 'I forget how many people rang us up this morning,

Alix for one, who wants to start her work apparently.'

Diaries, 9 October 1917

'We started printing in earnest after lunch, and Alix came punctually; was instructed, and left on her high stool while we took the air with Tinkler.'

Diaries, 16 October 1917

Unfortunately, Virginia reports in the same diary entry that after two hours, Alix found the work boring and wanted to give it up: 'The idea weighed upon her and I assured her there was no need for it to weigh.'[6] It is also interesting to note that in the above entry, Virginia misspells Tinker the dog's name, as it is replaced by 'Tinkler'.

Even with these issues with assistants, the printing process had to continue, as they were still in the middle of making Katherine Mansfield's *Prelude*. During this time, Virginia often found herself in bed during menstruation (she often called it being 'recumbent'), but still was encouraged by the thought of working on the press:

'This is much mitigated by printing, which I do from my bed on the sloping table. We took off a proof of 2 pages, on paper of the right size and liked the looks of it immensely. Our paper will be soft and yellow tinted.'

Diaries, 25 October 1917

It seems that Virginia intended to keep working on the Hogarth Press publications, even when she was feeling unwell. Her enthusiasm and desire to be closely involved in the printing process must have brought the couple closer together. The road to printing *Prelude* was not smooth, and the printing press the couple had bought seemed to cause them some problems:

'We began our printing off this afternoon. Our first discovery was the important one that the springs aren't even, or the balls different in weight. We – or L. – put this more or less right, and we printed 300 copies of the first page.'

Diaries, 13 November 1917

This would lead them to the conclusion that they would be better off buying another printing press, and this time, bought one from a local printer in Richmond, Mr McDermott. McDermott ran the Prompt Press just off The Green in the town, who Virginia called 'the little printer':

'We looked in, and spent half an hour, talking to the little printer, who has 2 machines and 1 press for sale. The difficulty is to decide; but probably we shall buy one.'

Diaries, 14 November 1917

'We printed off another page, very successfully, which took till tea time, and then we went round in the semi-darkness to the little printer, who will come round any moment now to see the room for the press.'

Diaries, 15 November 1917

'The little printer came round at the end of the last page, and stayed perhaps 1 hour…We have advanced £10, and for that bought the cutting press, and stipulated that the printing press shall be here by Jan. 14th.'

Diaries, 19 November 1917

By this time in November, the couple were in need of help at the Press, and so enlisted the help of Barbara Bagenal (née Hiles), who was a friend of Dora Carrington. Bagenal would later become a companion of Virginia's brother-in-law, Clive Bell. Barbara did not fare too well in the printing business, as the next few quotations demonstrate:

'It is quite impossible to write with Barbara taking her first lesson in printing, and Leonard mending the machine which has broken of course; but we did enjoy ourselves immensely.'

Letter to Lady Ottoline Morrell, 21 November 1917

'Anyhow on Wednesday Barbara came to make a start, and the machine thereupon completely struck work, one of the rollers being cut, and jibbing, and as our stock of K's ran out, she could only set 4 lines. This she did however, quickly and without fault, so that she promises well.'

Diaries, 22 November 1917

'We had Barbara here for 3 days, with disastrous results, for when we looked at her work, it was so full of faults we had to take it down.'

Diaries, 3 December 1917

Although Virginia was complimentary about Barbara and her account-keeping, it seemed that Barbara did not continue her work at the Press into January 1918 when the couple were still working on Katherine Mansfield's *Prelude*:

'We are hard at work printing a long story by a woman called Katherine Mansfield. I think it'll be out by Easter, and I shall come round with my wares like a peddlar. It's very good I think; but the publisher wouldn't take it.'

Letter to Violet Dickinson, 14 January 1918

'At this rate Katherine's story will be done in 5 weeks. We rather think of doing a little book of woodcuts, either after this book, or at the same time, on our small press.'

Diaries, 25 January 1918

As well as working hard on the lengthy process of *Prelude*, the couple were already thinking about what their next endeavour should be:

'It's a great nuisance having to go away just as we were at last getting ahead with our printing. Our next effort will be a book of woodcuts by Carrington and fables by Lytton Strachey. That I'm sure you'll like.'

Letter to Margaret Llewelyn Davies, 19 February 1918

Due to the complexity of printing, they sought help from McDermott who ran the Prompt Press. Indeed, he helped with the printing for Mansfield's *Prelude*. According to Leonard, McDermott struck up a friendship with the couple, which was to last the duration of their life in Richmond. However, McDermott '…produced one of the worst printed books ever published, certainly the worst ever published by the Hogarth Press.'[7]

Leonard and Virginia had discussed the possibility of publishing some of Virginia's short stories, and this was to become *Monday or Tuesday*. The printing of this publication was deemed too much for the couple to cope with, and so they asked McDermott to print it instead. Apparently, the choice of paper was completely wrong, and this ended up with having too much ink on the rollers. By allowing McDermott to publish one of their books, they departed from the idea of printing their books in-house, and thus they were on the road to becoming a professional publisher.

By June 1918, the couple were almost finished with their work on *Prelude*, which they would end up folding and glueing all through the following month as well. Despite the physical nature of the work, it's clear that the couple were still enjoying the process of printing:

> 'Leonard is working tremendously hard, and he spends all his spare time printing, which becomes more and more fascinating. We are just bargaining for a new press, which we shall put in the basement.'

Letter to Violet Dickinson, 10 June 1918

> 'The title page was finally done on Sunday. Now I'm in the fury of folding and stapling…By rights these processes should be dull; but it's always possible to devise some little skill or economy, and the pleasure of profiting by them keeps one content.'

Diaries, 9 July 1918

Katherine Mansfield's short story *Prelude* was finally published in July 1918. Around this time, Virginia was working on *Kew Gardens*, a short story inspired by the gardens of the same name near Hogarth House in south London. In a letter to her sister Vanessa, Virginia admitted that the story was '…very bad now, and not worth printing.'[8] In the same letter, Virginia urges her sister to illustrate the story, which, Vanessa agreed to do and the book was eventually published in 1919 with Vanessa's illustrations.

Virginia and T.S. Eliot had been corresponding for a short time in 1918 before finally meeting at Hogarth House in November. She describes him as '…intellectual, intolerant with strong views of his own and a poetic creed.'[9] Having been born in St. Louis, Eliot settled in England in 1915 after his marriage, and in a letter to Roger Fry, Virginia writes:

'We are asking Eliot to let us print a poem, and I've done a new short story, illustrated by Nessa.'

Letter to Roger Fry, 15 October 1918

This short story was of course *Kew Gardens* and the couple were to eventually publish Eliot's *Poems* in 1919. They were working on two publications simultaneously, their first effort to do so. Still heavily reliant on Vanessa, Virginia would write to her asking for advice:

'We're getting on with the printing. Have you any idea how many copies we ought to sell – what price could we ask?'

Letter to Vanessa Bell, 19 November 1918

This must refer to *Kew Gardens*, as *Poems* was not ready by this time in November. According to Leonard, *Kew Gardens* was put on sale at 2s and they printed 170 copies.[10] Eliot's *Poems* was priced at 2s. 6d with fewer than 250 copies printed. Of *Poems*, Virginia was particularly proud:

'Today we finished printing Eliot's poems – our best work so far by a long way, owing to the quality of the ink.'

Diaries, 19 March 1919

Both publications were published in May 1919, and this time they were thinking more about eliciting a critical response. Unlike *Two Stories*, they sent out review copies to organisations such as *The Times Literary Supplement*. In fact, the *Literary Supplement* published such an enthusiastic review of *Kew Gardens*, that when the couple returned to Hogarth House from Asheham in June:

'…we found the hall covered with envelopes and postcards containing orders from booksellers all over the country.'

Beginning Again:241

This led to a second printing of 500 copies of *Kew Gardens*, which the couple could not undertake themselves, and so enlisted the help of another printer. The success of Virginia's short story must have been extremely encouraging for the couple and showed Virginia that she could earn money from her writing without the help of outside publishers.

> 'The pleasure of success was considerably damaged, first by our quarrel, and second, by the necessity of getting some 90 copies ready, cutting covers, printing tables, glueing backs, and finally despatching, which used up all spare time and some not spare till this moment. But how success showered during those days! '

Diaries, 10 June 1919

This was surely a turning point in Virginia's career as a writer and publisher, and even Leonard himself wrote '*Kew Gardens* showed me that we could, if we wished, publish a book commercially and successfully'.[11] It seems very apt that the story which appears to change the fortunes of the couple was inspired by the gardens so close to their home in Richmond. It was clear with the success of *Kew Gardens* that the Hogarth Press was changing into something bigger, and so decisions needed to be made:

> 'What steps we're to take is not at the moment clear to me. Whether to become a shop or remain a small private press – whether to get help or refuse it.'

Diaries, 18 June 1919

'We're thinking of getting an office and a secretary…
and now we expect another rush of orders for Eliot
and Murry. I believe a poor man could make his
fortune out of this trade – but combined with editing,
reviews and writing novels, it's a little overwhelming.'

Letter to Dora Carrington, 18 June 1919

'I seem to spend my life in addressing envelopes. The
Hogarth Press is growing like a beanstalk, and we
think we must set up a shop and keep a clerk.'

Letter to Violet Dickinson, 13 July 1921

Even though Virginia was occasionally feeling a little
overwhelmed by the demands of running a commercial
enterprise, the success of their printing endeavour offered
them artistic control over their own work. Leonard
commented on this too:

'Publishing our *Two Stories* and Virginia's *Kew Gardens*
had shown us, and particularly Virginia, how pleasant
it is for a writer to be able to publish his own books.'

Downhill All the Way:68

As Leonard goes on to say, one of Virginia's afflictions
was the misery and horror of having to send her work to
publishers to be judged and valued. Her first book, *The
Voyage Out* was submitted to Gerald Duckworth, Virginia's
half-brother, who had not been the most positive of
influences in Virginia's early life. The idea that the couple
could publish Virginia's new novel, *Jacob's Room*, '…filled her
[Virginia] with delight, for she would thus avoid the misery
of submitting this highly experimental novel to the criticism
of Gerald Duckworth.'[12] It was also at this point that the
couple bought out the rights to *The Voyage Out* and *Night and*

Day from Duckworth, and Leonard's *The Village in the Jungle* from Edward Arnold, so that they would have complete control over their own work. One of the most telling quotations regarding how Virginia felt about the influence of the Press can be found in a diary entry in April 1921:

> 'What depresses me is the thought that I have ceased to interest people – at the very moment when, by help of the press, I thought I was becoming more myself.

Diaries, 8 April 1921

As a writer, Virginia both craved and resented being liked by other people, yet the Press was helping her to define herself. In a similar way to how she felt about Hogarth House when leaving, she humanises the Press:

> 'My apology for not writing is quite truthfully, the Hogarth Press… The Hogarth Press, you see, begins to outgrow its parents.'

Diaries, 25 November 1921

It is quite telling that she refers to being a parent of the Press, and the growth of the business certainly preoccupies the pair of them. The couple were not to have any children on the advice of Virginia's doctors and it's possible that the Hogarth Press was able to compensate in some way for the loss and sadness which they may have felt at this time about the prospect of being childless.

In 1920, the Woolfs were joined by Ralph [Reginald] Partridge as an assistant at the Press, but their relationship was stormy for the next three years. Ralph was in a complicated love triangle at the time, being married to Dora Carrington and friends with Lytton Strachey. Dora was in love with Lytton Strachey but Strachey was more interested in a relationship with Ralph. Initially, Ralph was to work with the couple two to three days per week:

> 'We dine in the drawing room – the dining room being given over to print and Ralph.'

Diaries, 17 July 1922

The Hogarth Press was expanding all the time, with Virginia's own *Monday or Tuesday* in 1921, and *Jacob's Room* published in 1922. *Jacob's Room* was the first full-length novel that the Press published and Virginia later admitted that it was the favourite of all her novels. The Woolfs needed Ralph to work more than three days a week, but he was unwilling to do so. Their working relationship with Ralph was becoming untenable, especially as the Press was attracting offers from other publishers to buy the business. Lytton Strachey was keen to help Ralph further his ambitions and offered to help establish a rival press which Ralph could run. Virginia becomes annoyed with Ralph towards the end of 1922:

> 'What did make my blood boil was your assumption that Leonard and I are quite ready to be bamboozled with a bargain which would destroy the character of the press for the sake of money or pride or convenience; and that you must protect its rights. After all we have given the press whatever character it may have, and if you're going to tell me that you care more about it than I do, or know better what's good for it, I must reply that you are a donkey. You will retaliate by telling me that I'm another to take your chance remarks seriously.'

Letter to Ralph Partridge, 10 November 1922

This bargain that Virginia writes about is likely to be the offer from Heinemann to enter into a sort of 'association', but this would then destroy the character of the Press that the couple had worked so hard to achieve:

> 'The Hogarth Press is in travail. Heinemanns made us
> a most flattering offer - to the effect that we should
> give us [sic] our brains and blood, and they would
> see to sales and ledgers…We are both very willing to
> come to this conclusion and have decided for freedom
> and a fight with great private glee.'

Diaries, 3 December 1922

In the above diary entry, Virginia writes about freedom, and this is exactly what the Hogarth Press in Richmond had given to her; the freedom to write what she wanted and then to publish it. This freedom would have disappeared if they were to take any offer that was made to them. The desire to keep her freedom also meant letting go of Ralph:

> 'So far as I can see, Ralph's disappearance would leave
> us more freedom, but give us more work. We should
> have to make further arrangements. But the basis
> would be sound, which is the great thing.'

Diaries, 15 December 1922

Ralph's working relationship with the couple had broken down by the beginning of 1923 and he must have known the writing was on the wall when they employed another assistant in January. Marjorie [Margery] Joad (née Thomson) had met the Woolfs while they were having discussions with Heinemann. She intended to become a printer and was invited to see their press, and was offered employment by them:

> 'Don't forget your play for the Hogarth Press. We are
> taking on a manager, and hope to become more and
> more professional.'

Letter to Hope Mirrlees, 6 January 1923

'You are the most faithful of subscribers. Many thanks for your cheque. Next week we start an all-time manager, and we become more and more full of works to print. I wish we had something of yours.'

Letter to Violet Dickinson, 23 January 1923

On February 7th 1923, it was the anniversary of Vanessa's marriage to Clive Bell, a day that Virginia hadn't forgotten. Virginia might have worried that she would lose her sister to a man when she left to get married. However, this had not happened, and Vanessa was still very much involved in Virginia's life. On this day in a diary entry, Virginia reflects on '...Joad's drawling voice and Ralph's stubbornness.'[13] as well as the following:

'I suppose the Press must now lose something of its charm and become more strenuous; acquiring let us hope a different charm.'

Diaries, 7 February 1923

Managing staff is never easy in a small business and the couple took the decision to let Ralph go in March, but they had the enthusiastic Marjorie [Margery] to help them:

'I must make out a work scheme. But for a moment I will dally with description. Margery is doing well, a sign of which is that we now scarcely notice her accent. If she were doing badly it would grate upon us intolerably. We are well up in our books.'

Diaries, 23 March 1923

Virginia was still in contact with Barbara Bagenal, who had helped them at the Press in the early years, and continued her praise of Marjorie [Margery]:

'Mrs Joad is doing very well - much better, to be

honest, than dear Ralph, but then she is a daily worker, enthusiastic, sanguine, and much impressed by small mercies. If only she didn't scent herself, rather cheaply, I should have nothing to say against her.'

Letter to Barbara Bagenal, 24 June 1923

In these last years in Richmond, the Press was still growing and becoming more demanding on both Leonard and Virginia, but it seems that the couple were still happy with what they were doing. Virginia alludes to the Press being similar to a child, yet again, in another letter to Barbara:

'One can't ever go away without some such reason. I assure you the Press is worse than 6 children at breast simultaneously. Consider the Sow. She shows no embarrassment. But Leonard and I live apart - he in the basement, I in the printing room. We meet only at meals, often so cross that we can't speak, and generally dirty. His triumphs always coincide with my disasters.

When one's up, the other's down.'

Letter to Barbara Bagenal, 8 July 1923

This devotion to the Press can be seen in other correspondence from Virginia as well as her diary. In 1923, the Hogarth Press was printing Eliot's *The Waste Land*:

'We had been hoping we might see you, but every weekend, save one, has been sacrificed to the Hogarth Press, which grows daily and hourly more exacting.'

Letter to Vita Sackville-West, July 1923

'As for the press, we have finished Tom, much to our relief. He will be published this August by Marjorie; and altogether we have worked at full speed since May.

And that is I'm persuaded the root and source and origin of all health and happiness.'

Diaries, 28 July 1923

By the time that the couple decided to leave Richmond for Bloomsbury in 1924, the Hogarth Press was well-established as a successful literary and commercial enterprise. They would continue to publish books in their new home in Tavistock Square but Richmond had been the birthplace of Virginia's 'child' and that fact would never change in her mind.

Virginia and Leonard Woolf printed and published around 32 books in the Richmond incarnation of the Hogarth Press. *In Downhill All the Way*[14], Leonard provides a list of the publications completed during the Richmond era:

1917	*Two Stories* by Leonard and Virginia Woolf
1918	*Prelude* by Katherine Mansfield
1919	*Poems* by T.S. Eliot
	Kew Gardens by Virginia Woolf
	Critic in Judgment by J. Middleton Murry
1920	*Story of the Siren* by E.M. Forster
	Paris by Hope Mirrlees
	Gorky's *Reminiscences of Tolstoi*
	Stories from the Old Testament by Logan Pearsall Smith
1921	*Monday or Tuesday* by Virginia Woolf
	Stories from the East by Leonard Woolf
	Poems by Clive Bell
	Tchekhov's *Notebooks*
1922	*Jacob's Room* by Virginia Woolf
	Stavrogin's Confession by Dostoevsky
	The Gentlemen from San Francisco by

Bunin
Autobiography of Countess Tolstoi
Daybreak by Fredegond Shove
Karn by Ruth Manning-Sanders
1923   *Pharos and Pharillon* by E.M. Forster
Woodcuts by Roger Fry
Sampler of Castile by Roger Fry
The Waste Land by T.S. Eliot
The Feather Bed by Robert Graves
Mutations of the Phoenix by Herbert Read
Legend of Monte della Sibilla by Clive Bell
Poems by Ena Limebeer
Tolstoi's *Love Letters*
Talks with Tolstoi by A.V. Goldenveiser
Letters of Stephen Reynolds
The Dark by Leonid Andreev
When it was June by Mrs Lowther

Standouts from the above list include many of their Bloomsbury associates, such as Roger Fry and Clive Bell, as well as major works by Mansfield and Eliot. When they first started hand printing a pamphlet on their dining room table, the couple probably couldn't imagine just how important the literary contribution of the Hogarth Press would be to modernist English Literature.

The impact of the Hogarth Press on Virginia as an individual is hard to quantify, but it is safe to say that it gave her greater confidence to express herself as a writer without worrying about what others thought of her. The Press also provided the freedom of being able to control the entire creative process from conception to end product, and the experience of reading and editing the work of other writers must have provided insight into the writing process too. By 1938, Virginia was well-established as a writer, and after twenty years, she finally relinquished her interest in the Press. It was carried on by Leonard Woolf and John Lehmann until 1946, when it became part of the Chatto and Windus group. The Hogarth Press published more than 500 titles between its inception and 1946.

Woolf on Writing

So far of course, the success is much more than we expected. I think I am better pleased so far than I have ever been.

Diaries, 29 October 1922

Virginia's first novel had been started as early as 1908 and was initially called *Melymbrosia*. She wanted to capture the 'flight of the mind' but wasn't sure how to write about it. In 1910, she visited an art exhibition, featuring the paintings of Manet, Cezanne and Picasso and was inspired by their work to continue trying to write her novel. In it, the character of Rachel Vinrace sets out on an excursion to South America. The character's journey reflects the psychological exploration which Virginia was attempting into the unchartered territory of the subconscious mind. She changed the title to *The Voyage Out* and following many heavy revisions, the novel was finished in 1912 but the strain of completing the novel led to a mental collapse so its publication was delayed until 1915, when it was thought that Virginia had recovered sufficiently to withstand the reviews. Like any other debut novelist, Virginia was anxious about how people would respond to her work and she sought feedback from her most loyal friends, and one, in particular – Lytton Strachey:

> 'Your praise is far the nicest of any I've had...you almost give me courage to read it, which I've not done

since it was printed, and I wonder how it would strike me now. I suspect your criticism about the failure of conception is quite right. I think I had a conception, but I don't think it made itself felt. What I wanted to do was to give the feeling of a vast tumult of life, as various and disorderly as possible, which should be cut short for the moment by the death and go on again – and the whole was to have a sort of pattern and be somehow controlled. The difficulty was to keep any sort of coherence, - also to give enough detail to make the characters interesting – which Forster says I didn't do. I really wanted three volumes. Do you think it is impossible to get this sort of effect in a novel; - is the result bound to be too scattered to be intelligible? I expect one will learn to get more control in time.'

Letter to Lytton Strachey, 28 February 1916

It was not uncommon for Virginia to avoid reading her work once it was fully completed; it seemed to affect her rather negatively. Although 1916 was a relatively quiet year for Virginia in terms of writing, it has been suggested that she had already started her second novel, *Night and Day*. This was to be her longest novel, and it shows a return to a more realist style. During 1917, Virginia and Leonard were busy setting up the Hogarth Press and Virginia was working on a short story, *The Mark on the Wall*, which was to feature along with Leonard's story titled *Three Jews*, both of which were published in 1917.

'We both notice that lately we've written at a terrific pace: L 40,000 words & as yet hasn't touched the book itself; I'm well past 100,000.'

Diaries, 12 March 1918

Virginia was well aware that she wanted to be liked as a

writer and was fearful of negative reviews. Yet, even at this relatively early stage in her writing career, she was sure that this is what she was destined to do:

> 'It's the curse of a writer's life to want praise so much, & to be cast down by blame, or indifference. The only sensible course is to remember that writing is after all what one does best.'

> Diaries, 3 November 1918

Virginia used her diaries as writing practice and many times described how she was feeling regarding her writing; showing her frustration or pleasure with her progress, almost as if she was leaving herself reminders of how she could complete her writing:

> 'I keep thinking of different ways to manage my scenes; conceiving endless possibilities; seeing life, as I walk about the streets, an immense opaque block of material to be conveyed by me into its equivalent of language.'

> Diaries, 4 November 1918

After *Two Stories* was published by the couple in 1917, the next work of fiction that Virginia published was *Kew Gardens*, inspired by the gardens that were so close to her home in Richmond. *Kew Gardens*, called by some a 'sketch', mainly follows the moments of four couples: a married couple with their children who are reminiscing about past times in the gardens; an old man and his friend William, talking about the First World War, a couple of women aimlessly talking; and a young couple in love. The narrative also focuses on insects and small animals such as snails as the story takes us through each moment with the couples. This could be seen to be reminiscent of *The Mark on the Wall* when the mark was revealed to be a snail:

> 'In the oval flower-bed the snail, whose shell had
> been stained red, blue and yellow for the space of
> two minutes or so, now appeared to be moving very
> slightly in its shell.'

Kew Gardens[1]

As the couple lived near to Kew Gardens, Virginia often visited them, sometimes alone or with Leonard, but occasionally with friends. On November 26th 1917, she writes that they went to Kew and:

> '…saw a blazing bush, as red as cherry blossom, but
> more intense – frostily red – also gulls rising and falling
> for pieces of meat, their crowd waved aside suddenly
> by three very elegant grey cranes.'

Diaries, 26 November 1917

Kew Gardens was the second of Virginia's works to be published by the Hogarth Press. It was finished and printed in 1918 and published in May 1919. In a diary entry dated December 17th 1918, Virginia writes: 'We have printed off the text of *Kew Gardens*.'[2] Upon publication, Virginia was less than impressed with *Kew Gardens*, calling it 'slight and short' and leaving her wondering why Leonard liked it so much.[3] She even went back to read *The Mark on the Wall* and found problems with that. Every writer has to have an inner critic to be able to edit their own work. Ernest Hemingway referred to this (in an interview with the literary editor George Plimpton) as 'a built-in, shock-proof, shit detector. This is the writer's radar and all great writers have had it.' Virginia's inner critic could be harsh. In reference to *Kew Gardens*, she writes:

> '…the worst of writing is that one depends so much

on praise. I feel rather sure that I shall get none for this story; and I shall mind a little.'

Diaries, 12 May 1919

Virginia's self-deprecation was unnecessary as *Kew Gardens* was a success, mostly down to the favourable review it received in the *Literary Supplement*, which led to the couple being inundated with orders for the short story.

'All these orders…come from a review in the Lit. Sup…in which as much praise was allowed me as I like to claim. And 10 days ago I was stoically facing complete failure!'

Diaries, 10 June 1919

In the same diary entry, Virginia reports that she had received a letter from the publisher Macmillan in the U.S saying that they enjoyed *The Voyage Out* and wished to read a copy of *Night and Day*. It seemed that the success of *Kew Gardens* had given her writing career the boost it needed to become successful.

During her time in Richmond, she often compared her first novel *The Voyage Out* published in 1915, with her second novel, *Night and Day*, which was published in 1919. In both Virginia and Leonard's memories, it was clear that she found the process of writing her first novel most difficult, often writing and rewriting it numerous times.

'In my own opinion [*Night and Day*] is a much more mature & finished & satisfactory book than *The Voyage Out*, as it has reason to be… And yet I can't help thinking that, English fiction being what it is, I compare for originality & sincerity rather well with most of the moderns.'

Diaries, 27 March 1919

Referring back to the entry in which Virginia stated that she avoided reading her work once it was printed, she muses on whether she will be able to do the same with *Night and Day*, seeing as it was a much more pleasant work to write than her earlier effort:

> 'I don't suppose I've ever enjoyed any writing so much as I did the last half of N&D. I wonder if I shall ever be able to read it again? Is the time coming when I can endure to read my own writing in print without blushing and shivering and wishing to take cover?'

Diaries, 27 March 1919

Virginia often used her diary to reflect on the process of her writing, but she was affected by her grammatical mistakes and the 'rough, random style of it.'[4] It was here that she stated that her future self was forbidden to '… let the eye of man behold it.' Yet, even though she might have been embarrassed by her personal writing, it is the regular writing in her diary to which Virginia attributes her professional success:

> 'But what is more to the point is my belief that the habit of writing thus for my own eye only is good practise… I believe that during the past year I can trace some increase of ease in my professional writing which I attribute to my casual half hours after tea.'

Diaries, 20 April 1919

The diary, which she had begun so early in her life, was now helping her to refine her writing skills in her professional life. It is unclear whether Virginia ever intended her personal writing to be for public reading. Certainly in the above diary entry, her view is that her diary was written for her eyes only, and this is echoed in her last letter to Leonard.

Night and Day was the second, and longest, of her novels. The novel follows five people, including Katharine Hilbery and Ralph Denham, as they tussle with love, marriage and work in early twentieth century London. It is considered the most 'plotted' of Virginia's novels, echoing the 'traditional' novel that Virginia was to eschew with her following work. The writing was clearly influenced by the area in which she lived, using places nearby as locations in the book:

> 'At a quarter-past three in the afternoon of the following Saturday Ralph Denham sat on the bank of the lake in Kew Gardens, dividing the dial-plate of his watch into sections with his forefinger.'

Night and Day[5]

Virginia liked to walk along the towpath beside the river Thames, while she was in Richmond:

> '...the broad green space, the vista of trees, with the ruffled gold of the Thames in the distance and the Ducal castle standing in its meadows.'

Night and Day[6]

The time between finishing a novel and its public reception could be a torment for Virginia, in spite of her protestations to the contrary in this letter:

> 'Turning, however, to the immediate present, I see that *Night and Day* will be out shortly...I don't feel nervous; nobody cares a hang what one writes, and novels are such clumsy and half extinct monsters at the best; but, oh dear, what a bore it will be!'

Letter to Katherine Arnold-Forster, 9 October 1919

It seems disingenuous of Virginia to appear so casual about her work, as it was clear that she cared a great deal about what people thought of it. However, with this particular publication, Virginia displayed more confidence than usual:

> 'In the first place, there it is, out and done with; then I read a bit and liked it; then I have a kind of confidence, that the people whose judgement I value will probably think well of it, which is much reinforced by the knowledge that even if they don't, I shall pick up and start another story on my own…but on the whole, I see what I'm aiming at; what I feel is that this time I've had a fair chance and done my best.'

Diaries, 21 October 1919

Once *Night and Day* had been published, it was only a matter of time before Virginia received the reviews. Virginia herself was 'more excited and pleased than nervous', and it was Clive Bell who got first word to the writer, calling it 'a work of genius'. Virginia responded in her diary with 'I own I'm pleased; yet not convinced that it is as he says.'[7] Clearly still disbelieving her friends, Virginia's wish for a review in *The Times* was granted:

> 'Then there's a column in the Times this morning; high praise; & intelligent too; saying among other things that [*Night and Day*] though it has less brilliance on the surface, has more depth than the other; with which I agree.'

Diaries, 30 October 1919

Her friend, Lady Ottoline Morrell had also reacted favourably to Virginia's newest publication:

> 'It was very good of you to write, and a great pleasure to me to think of your liking my book. I hoped you would; but one never knows. I tried to get a little

more 'beauty' into this one, and risked spoiling the 'originality'.'

Letter to Lady Ottoline Morrell, November 1919

In between writing her major works, Virginia also wrote reviews and essays for other publishers and journals. Although, Virginia Woolf had a privileged and wealthy family background, both she and Leonard had to earn enough money from their writing to supplement their joint annual income. For example, in 1919, Virginia had earned £153 from her writing and Leonard earned £578 from freelance articles, his books and his editorship at the *International Review*[8]. Their investment in the printing press and creation of a small publishing business may have been motivated by a desire to become more financially independent. In *Downhill All the Way*, Leonard confirms that between the years 1919 to 1924, Virginia was '...writing a considerable amount of journalism...She looked upon it usually as a method of making money.'[9] It is clear from her diaries and essays that she found this trying; attempting to write many reviews while also working on her own novels tended to be a balancing act:

'Shall I ever again get time for writing here? Never have I been so pressed with reviewing.'

Diaries, 1 November 1919

The reading and evaluation of other writers' works, may well have contributed to Virginia's growing confidence in herself and her literary judgement. Reading back over her own diary at the end of 1919, she notices how she has grown as a person:

'Oh yes, I've enjoyed reading the past years diary, and shall keep it up. I'm amused to find how its grown a person, with almost a face of its own.'

Diaries, 28 December 1919

The discipline of committing your thoughts to paper on a daily basis is still regarded as a good way to practise your craft as a writer. Through her regular diary writing, Virginia honed her composition and sentence writing skills as well as gaining access to her creative self. It has been claimed that a lot of Virginia's fiction has a basis in real life events. Take Katharine Hilbery, for example; Virginia herself admitted that the character was based on her sister, Vanessa; '...try thinking of Katharine as Vanessa, not me.'[10] Upon discussing Marjorie Strachey's writing, Virginia muses:

> 'I wonder, parenthetically, whether I too, deal thus openly in autobiography & call it fiction?'

Diaries, 14 January 1920

Even though Virginia's professional writing was starting to get noticed, she was still experimenting with different techniques and literary devices. This, however, was starting to become clearer and is a theme commonly found in her diaries:

> 'My hope it that I've learnt my business sufficiently now to provide all sorts of entertainments. Anyhow, there's no doubt the way lies somewhere in that direction; I must still grope & experiment but this afternoon I had a gleam of light. Indeed, I think from the ease with which I'm developing the unwritten novel there must be a path for me there.'

Diaries, 26 January 1920

Her feelings about her writing fluctuated between positivity and self-doubt, as the next two quotations demonstrate, written only a few months apart:

> 'I fancy old Virginia, putting on spectacles to read of March 1920 will decidedly wish me to continue. Greetings! My dear ghost; and take heed that I don't think 50 a very great age. Several good books can be written still; and here's the bricks for a fine one.'

Diaries, 9 March 1920

> 'It is worth mentioning, for future reference, that the creative power which bubbles so pleasantly on beginning a new book quiets down after a time, and one goes on more steadily. Doubts creep in…I am a little anxious.'

Diaries, 11 May 1920

It was around this time that Virginia was working on her first collection of short stories, eventually to be titled *Monday or Tuesday.* According to Leonard, *Monday or Tuesday* was the start of the time of '…crucial importance in her development as a novelist.'[11] She wrote the short stories between 1917 and 1921, and Leonard called them a prelude to *Jacob's Room.* The short story collection contained eight of Virginia's stories, some of which had been published before:

A Haunted House
A Society
Monday or Tuesday
An Unwritten Novel
The String Quartet
Blue & Green
Kew Gardens
The Mark on the Wall

As well as writing and revising the short stories for *Monday or Tuesday*, Virginia started work on *Jacob's Room* in

April 1920; 'I'm planning to begin *Jacob's Room* next week with luck. (That's the first time I've written that.)'[12] Even though Virginia was extremely busy with reviewing, her new novel and the short stories, it was apparent that she was enjoying her newest work of fiction:

> 'I get on with Jacob – the most amusing novel writing I've done, I think; in the doing I mean.'

Diaries, 20 May 1920

The progress on *Jacob's Room* was most likely hindered due to her reviewing work, as Virginia was finding less time to work on her own writing:

> 'I'm getting doubtful whether I shall have time to write the story called *Monday or Tuesday* – if not, I don't know what to call the book.'

Letter to Vanessa Bell, 31 October 1920

However, on 7th April 1921, her book of short stories, *Monday or Tuesday*, was published, but the couple were not happy with the printing which McDermott had done for them; '…my book [*Monday or Tuesday*] out (prematurely) and nipped, a damp firework.'[13], but she expands on the problem in a letter:

> 'We are much ashamed of the printing of my one. We were persuaded to let a little printer [McDermott] here try his hand at it, and he has produced an odious object, which leaves black stains wherever it touches.'

Letter to Violet Dickinson, April 1921

In addition to this problem with the publication, Virginia was certain that the book of short stories would not do very well: 'I much doubt if [*Monday or Tuesday*] will sell 500, or cover expenses. But I want to push on with it nevertheless.'[14]

Despite her misgivings about the book, she did receive favourable comments from friends:

> 'And Eliot astounded me by praising *Monday or Tuesday*!
> This really delighted me…. It pleases me to think that
> I could discuss my writing openly with him.'

Diaries, 7 June 1921

It is at this point in the diaries that Virginia first mentions *The Common Reader* (provisionally titled *Reading* by Virginia). This was to be a collection of essays, revising some previously written ones and working on some new essays. Although not published until 1925, she had started the preparation process:

> 'I must start *Reading*. Directly I've started *Reading* I
> shall think of another novel, I daresay. So that the only
> question appears to be – will my fingers stand so much
> scribbling?'

Diaries, 15 November 1921

It seems that Virginia only believes now that she is writing work of worth, even with the success of publications such as *Kew Gardens*:

> 'Writing is still like heaving bricks over a wall… I've
> wasted 5 whole years (I count) doing it [lying in bed];
> so you must call me 35 – not 40 – and expect rather
> less of me. Not that I haven't picked up something
> from my insanities and all the rest. Indeed, I suspect
> they've done instead of religion.'

Letter to E.M. Forster, 21 January 1922

With this letter extract, she believes that being ill has actually given her something to work with for her fiction, and this can be connected, in part, to her essay *On Being*

Ill, published in 1926. Whether the above quotation can be seen to be a veiled attempt at encouragement or enthusiasm for her writing, Virginia was hit by a fairly negative review of *Monday or Tuesday* and this resulted in a rather pained diary entry in February 1922:

> 'It seems as if I succeed nowhere. Yet, I'm glad to find, I have acquired a little philosophy. It amounts to a sense of freedom. I write what I like writing & there's an end to it. Moreover, heaven knows I get consideration enough… I meant to write about death, only life came breaking in as usual. I like, I see, to question people about death. I have taken it into my head that I shan't live till 70.'

Diaries, 17 February 1922

This feeling of negativity continued into the following day's entry:

> 'I have made up my mind that I'm not going to be popular, and so genuinely that I look upon disregard or abuse as part of my bargain. I'm to write what I like; and they're to say what they like. My only interest as a writer lies, I begin to see, in some queer individuality.'

Diaries, 18 February 1922

Yet, Virginia needed to continue writing as she was working on more than one new publication simultaneously. *Jacob's Room* and *The Common Reader* were still yet to be completed. The negative feeling passed relatively quickly, when in the following month, Virginia reported:

> 'I am writing the first chapter of *Reading* with the usual fabulous zest. I have never enjoyed any writing more. How often have I said this? Does the pleasure last?'

Diaries, 24 March 1922

As well as working on *The Common Reader*, Virginia was nearing the end of work on *Jacob's Room*, which follows the story of Jacob Flanders, a character who is representative of the Edwardian values that led the country into war. Critics have described it not only as an elegy for the fallen men of the war, but also for Virginia's brother, Thoby.

> 'The strange thing about life is that though the nature of it must have been apparent to every one for hundreds of years, no one has left any adequate account of it.'

Jacob's Room[15]

Prior to publication, it was usual for Leonard to read through Virginia's manuscript, and with *Jacob's Room*, this was no different:

> 'On Sunday L read through *Jacob's Room*. He thinks it my best work. But his first remark was that it was amazingly well written. We argued about it. He calls it a work of genius; he thinks it unlike any other novel.'

Diaries, 26 July 1922

High praise indeed from Leonard, which must have been very encouraging for Virginia. In the same diary entry, the reader sees confidence from Virginia unlike any seen before:

> 'There's no doubt in my mind that I have found out how to begin (at 40) to say something in my own voice; and that interests me so that I feel I can go ahead without praise.'

Diaries, 26 July 1922

This optimism must also have been buoyed by the news from Harcourt Brace, Virginia's publishers in the U.S, which she reported in her diary in October:

'We think *Jacob's Room* an extraordinarily distinguished and beautiful work. You have, of course, your own method, and it is not easy to foretell how many readers it will have; surely it will have enthusiastic ones, and we delight in publishing it.'

Diaries, 4 October 1922

In contrast to her earlier feelings of not wanting to, or avoiding, reading her own work, the probable success of *Jacob's Room* allowed her to think a little differently:

'At last, I like reading my own writing. It seems to me to fit me closer than it did before. I have done my task here better than I expected.'

Diaries, 4 October 1922

In the last few months before *Jacob's Room* was published, Virginia had started work on yet another work of fiction incorporating a character she had used before, namely Mrs Dalloway. It seems clear that *Mrs Dalloway in Bond Street* was intended to be the first chapter of the novel which was to become *Mrs Dalloway* (provisionally titled *The Hours* by Virginia). Take a look at the respective first lines from each publication:

'Mrs Dalloway said she would buy the gloves herself.'

Mrs Dalloway in Bond Street[16]

'Mrs Dalloway said she would buy the flowers herself.'

Mrs Dalloway[17]

It was apparent at this time that Virginia was starting to struggle somewhat. Her continual reference to water is evident in the following diary entry, in which she also comments on the importance of *Jacob's Room* on her writing:

> I want to be through the splash and swimming in calm
> water again. I want to be writing unobserved. Mrs
> Dalloway has branched into a book… and to be more
> close to the fact than Jacob: but I think Jacob was a
> necessary step, for me, in working free.

Diaries, 14 October 1922

In order to get back to calm water, Virginia had to survive
the reviews of *Jacob's Room* which was published on October
27th 1922. In a letter to David Garnett (Bunny), she admits
that she had doubts about her newest publication:

> One has so many doubts about one's books – about
> this one in particular I was doubtful whether it did
> keep together as a whole. So I am very much relieved
> by your saying that it does. But how far can one convey
> character without realism? That is my problem – one
> of them at least.

Letter to David Garnett, 20 October 1922

The doubt that Virginia had about *Jacob's Room* was not
aided by a review in *The Times* which seemed to attack
her characterisation, yet the novel had sold 650 copies by
this time and was being considered for a second edition.
However, the popularity of the novel among her readers did
not seem to alleviate Virginia's pessimism:

> I shall never write a book that is an entire success.
> This time the reviews are against me, and the private
> people enthusiastic. Either I am a great writer
> or a nincompoop… I don't want to be totting up
> compliments and comparing reviews. I want to think
> out *Mrs Dalloway*.

Diaries, 29 October 1922

She was still feeling this way in the following month:

'The reviews have said more against me than for me - on the whole. It's so odd how little I mind - and odd how little I care much that Clive thinks it a masterpiece. Yet the private praise has been the most whole hearted I've yet had.'

Diaries, 7 November 1922

However, only days later, Virginia was encouraged by more favourable reviews and seems to be perfectly happy with what she has achieved, mentioning in a later entry that *Jacob's Room* had sold more copies than before:

'Reviews are now favourable and utterly contradictory, as usual. I am quite able to write away without bother from self-consciousness...On the whole, I am perfectly satisfied, though; more so, I think, than ever before.'

Diaries, 13 November 1922

'Jacob has now sold 850 copies, and the second edition won't come much before it is needed I hope. People – my friends I mean – seem agreed that it is my masterpiece, and the starting point for fresh adventures.'

Diaries, 27 November 1922

The beginning of 1923 started badly for Virginia, with the upsetting news of the death of her friend and literary rival, Katherine Mansfield, whose *Prelude* was the second publication of the Hogarth Press. This appeared to affect Virginia in a way that she had not expected:

'When I began to write, it seemed to me there was no point in writing. Katherine won't read it. Katherine's my rival no longer. More generously I felt, but though I can do this better than she could, where is she, who could do what I can't!'

Diaries, 16 January 1923

In a similar way to the deaths of her parents, Virginia visualised Katherine and perhaps it was because Katherine was a young woman, a talented writer and an independent spirit that her death hit Virginia harder than than the deaths of some of her other acquaintances. Through this period, however, Virginia was still receiving good news about *Jacob's Room*:

'Jacob has gone into his second edition and is going to be translated into French. (This is dreadful boasting).'

Letter to Violet Dickinson, 23 January 1923

In a letter to Philip Morrell on February 3rd 1938, she wrote '...your liking *Jacob's Room*: my own favourite, the only one I can sometimes read a page of without disgust.'[18]. Even though this must have been encouraging, Virginia was still reeling from Mansfield's death:

'A certain melancholy has been brooding over me this fortnight. I date it from Katherine's death. The feeling so often comes to me now – Yes. Go on writing of course: but into emptiness. There's no competitor. I'm cock – a lonely cock whose crowing nothing breaks of my walk. For our friendship had so much that was writing in it. However, then I had my fever, and violent cold, was in and out of bed for a week, and still am below normal, I think.'

Diaries, 28 January 1923

Virginia, though, was still in the process of writing *The Hours*, but gained encouragement, as reported in her diary:

> 'Morgan told me that when he and Mortimer discussed novelists the other day they agreed that Lawrence and I were the only two whose future interested them. They think of my next book, which I think of calling 'The Hours', with excitement. This does encourage me.'

Diaries, 12 May 1923

This was certainly the encouragement that Virginia needed; she seemed to attack the writing of *The Hours* with vigour:

> 'I am a great deal interested suddenly in my book. I want to bring in the despicableness of people like Ott: I want to give the slipperiness of the soul. I have been too tolerant often. The truth is people scarcely care for each other. They have this insane instinct for life. But they never become attached to anything outside themselves.'

Diaries, 4 June 1923

Once more, while writing a significant novel, Virginia appears to question her writing ability and how she formulates her ideas into a coherent form:

> 'But now what do I feel about my writing? – this book, that is, *The Hours*, if that's its name? One must write from deep feeling, said Dostoevsky. And do I? Or do I fabricate with words, loving them as I do? No I think not. In this book I have almost too many ideas. I want to give life and death, sanity and insanity; I want to criticise the social system, and to show it at work, at its most intense – But here I may be posing…. But to go on. Am I writing *The Hours* from deep emotion? Of course, the mad part tries me so much, makes my

mind squint so badly that I can hardly face spending the next weeks at it...'

Diaries, 19 June 1923

The year 1923 was also the time when Virginia was working on *Freshwater*, which would be her only drama. The original idea for this had surfaced as early as 1919, but she didn't seem to start writing until perhaps she needed a break from the seriousness of *The Hours*. It was apparent that she found it easier to write than her novels:

'I wish I could write *The Hours* as freely and vigourously as I scribble *Freshwater*, a comedy. It's a strange thing how arduous I find my novels; and yet *Freshwater* is only spirited fun; and *The Hours* has some serious merit.'

Diaries, 8 July 1923

The age of 40 is commonly seen as a milestone, when a person is more than half-way through their life. It seems to have been a recurring theme in Virginia's diaries, with the sense of time running out to achieve her literary ambitions:

'My theory is that at 40 one either increases the pace or slows down. Needless to say which I desire. But, to be just, my activity is also mental. I'm working variously and with intention...In five years, I shall have fagged out a good book from it, I hope.'

Diaries, 28 July 1923

Freshwater was named after the town on the Isle of Wight where her great-aunt, the photographer Julia Margaret Cameron had a house, and features her great-aunt's circle of artistic and literary friends. It was a satirical play about the need for artistic freedom and escape from Victorian attitudes. It not only featured her great-aunt as a character, but also the actress Ellen Terry, who leaves her elderly husband and runs off to Bloomsbury with a younger man in the play. However, Virginia wasn't able to complete the play to her satisfaction at this time:

> 'On thinking over the play, I rather doubt it's worth going on with. It seemed to me, when I read it last night, that it's so much of a burlesque, and really rather too thin and flat to be worth getting people together at infinite trouble to act.'

Letter to Vanessa Bell, October 1923

Virginia reused her research about her aunt in an essay published in 1925 titled *Pattledom* but didn't revise the play until 1935. It was performed once during her lifetime by her family and friends in her sister's art studio in Fitzroy Street in 1935, directed by Virginia herself. The play was found in Leonard Woolf's papers after his death in 1969 and published in 1976, since when it has been translated into a number of languages and produced several times.

Her last few months in Richmond and at Hogarth House were mainly concerned with finding a new place to live in Bloomsbury, but throughout this time, she was still working on *The Hours* (later to become the novel *Mrs Dalloway*):

> 'I wrote the 100th page today… It took me a year's groping to discover what I call my tunnelling process, by which I tell the past by instalments, as I have need of it…I own I have my hopes for this book. I am going on writing it now till, honestly, I can't write another line.

Diaries, 15 October 1923

> I'm working at *The Hours* and think it a very interesting attempt; I may have found my mine this time I think.

I may get all my gold out. The great thing is never to feel bored with one's own writing. That is the signal for a change - never mind what, so long as it brings interest. And my vein of gold lies so deep, in such bent channels. To get it I must forge ahead, stoop and grope. But it is gold of a kind I think. Morgan said I had got further into the soul in *Jacob's Room* than any other novelist.'

Diaries, 9 February 1924

As demonstrated in this chapter, Virginia's life in Richmond was a prolific writing period which culminated in *Mrs Dalloway* (with a working title of *The Hours*), being published in 1925. Significantly, her time in the town had given her the creative freedom to experiment with her writing and the ability, through the Hogarth Press, to publish her own work without fear of criticism from editors or publishers. Following on from *Mrs Dalloway* in 1925, she also wrote the most well-known of her novels:

To the Lighthouse, 1927
Orlando: A Biography, 1928
The Waves, 1931
Flush: A Biography, 1933
The Years, 1937
Between the Acts, 1941 (posthumously published)

Among her numerous short stories and essays, other important works include the pacifist *Three Guineas* (1938) which was probably inspired by the death of her nephew Julian Bell in the Spanish Civil war, *Roger Fry: A Biography* (1940) and her seminal work, *A Room of One's Own*, published in 1929. The most famous quote from the book is undoubtedly:

'A woman must have money and a room of her own if

VIRGINIA WOOLF IN RICHMOND

she is to write fiction.'

In this extended essay, Virginia argues that without money, a woman cannot have the private space necessary to think and be creative. She refutes the argument that women produce inferior literary works, by claiming that their household duties and financial dependence on their husbands, limit their ability to compete on an equal basis with men. She also argues that room must be made for women's work in the male literary tradition. The essay was based on two lectures which Virginia gave to women at Cambridge University and it became an important feminist text for its insight into the unequal treatment of men and women in society. Virginia Woolf too has since become an important figure in feminist literary discourse.

This book is just one of hundreds which has been published about Virginia's life and work since her death. It has been made possible by drawing on Virginia's many volumes of diaries and letters which were published posthumously. This raises the question of whether an author's private papers should be published without their consent. Virginia probably never intended her diaries and letters to be published and she asked Leonard to destroy all her papers in the final line of her last letter to him:

'Dearest,

I want to tell you that you have given me complete happiness. No one could have done more than you have done. Please believe that. But I know that I shall never get over this: and I am wasting your life. It is this madness. Nothing anyone says can persuade me. You can work, and you will be much better without me. You see I can't write this even, which shows I am right. All I want to say is that until this disease came on we were perfectly happy. It was all due to you. No one could have been so good as you have been, from the very first day till now. Everyone knows that.'

V.

You will find Roger's letters to the Maurons in the writing table drawer in the Lodge. Will you destroy all my papers.'

In some of her last letters, she describes *Between the Acts* as a work she was not proud of, and says that it should not be published. It could be argued that she was referring to this manuscript as 'her papers' but it too was published shortly after her death in 1941, presumably with Leonard Woolf's permission.

The diaries themselves are now housed in the Berg Collection at the New York Public Library, where they have been since 1970. The first volume of her diary was published in 1977. The diaries were edited by Anne Olivier Bell, who had married Vanessa's son, Quentin. The publication of her diaries and letters have provided important material for scholars and writers to explore to gain a greater understanding of Virginia's mind and literary process. They have undoubtedly contributed over the years to Woolf's legacy. Her ability to reflect the 'flight of the mind' in the style of a 'stream of consciousness' in her writing established her, alongside James Joyce, as one of the co-founders of Modernist literature. Her struggle to make a name for herself as a respected writer in a male-dominated world, continues to inspire today.

Family in the Richmond Era

I greatly envy your brats. They are very interesting.

Letter to Vanessa Bell, 30 July 1916

Virginia Woolf's family background was complicated. One of her greatest influences was her mother, Julia Prinsep Stephen, who was born in India in 1846, and moved to England a few years later. She married Herbert Duckworth in 1867 and they had three children – George, Stella and Gerald. Following the death of her husband, she agreed to marry a widower, Leslie Stephen, in 1878. They went on to have another four children together – Vanessa, Thoby, Virginia and Adrian. Unfortunately, after contracting influenza, Julia died in 1895.

In her autobiographical writings, Virginia wrote about the heartache of losing her mother. *Reminiscences*, which was begun in 1907 as a sketch of Vanessa, states 'If what I have said of her has any meaning, you will believe that her death was the greatest disaster that could happen.'[1] Virginia continues to say that the dead usually become forgotten, but in the case of her mother, she often sees her, hears her laugh and is often closer than any of the living.

> 'The day mother died twenty something years ago. The smell of wreaths in the hall is always in the first flowers still; without remembering the day I was

thinking of her, as I often do – as good a memorial as one could wish.'

Diaries, 5 May 1919

A much later autobiographical piece, *A Sketch of the Past*, was started in 1939. According to many scholars, this is the most honest and open of Virginia's autobiographical works. Here, she describes her mother as being the centre of the family and she recalls the day that she died – May 5th 1895. 'Keep yourself straight, my little Goat.' were the last words Virginia heard her mother say to her. She describes that everything had come to an end after her mother's passing, but she '…got a feeling of calm, sadness and finality.'[2]

Leslie Stephen, born in 1832, was known as a man of letters, publishing many articles on religious concepts as well as becoming the first editor of the *Dictionary of National Biography*. He had previously been married to Harriet Thackeray and had one daughter, Laura. Harriet died in 1875, and Leslie went on to marry Julia three years later. Once again, in *Sketch of the Past*, Virginia recalls the memories of her father; '…a strong mind; an impatient, limited mind; a conventional mind entirely accepting his own standard of what is honest, what is moral…'.[3] However, Virginia also saw her father in violent rages, described as a 'beast' and trapped in a cage. According to her, he had disguised his own feelings for so long that he didn't know what they were anymore.

Towards the end of 1903, Leslie became extremely weak, and this continued into the first months of 1904. Virginia reports the condition of her father in her early letters to Violet Dickinson and Janet Case. Unfortunately, Leslie Stephen died on February 22nd 1904. In letters immediately following her father's death, Virginia writes: 'But how to go on without him, I don't know.'[4] In a similar way to how she felt about her mother's death, Virginia feels that her father is still with her: 'I have the curious feeling of living with him every day', she writes in a letter to Violet on March 4th 1904. Her father's death destabilised Virginia and her grief led to a serious mental collapse. She seems to have made an attempt at suicide by throwing herself out of a window in May 1904. She was medicated and briefly institutionalised under the care of her father's friend George Savage. She spent time recovering at the home of Violet Dickinson, who was a friend of her half-sister, Stella.

Vanessa (Nessa) born in 1879, was to be a huge part of Virginia's life, with numerous letters between the sisters often beginning with 'Dolphin', Virginia's pet name for Nessa. Vanessa was extremely important, with Virginia writing in 1931; 'I always feel I'm writing more for you than for anybody.'[5] An accomplished artist, Vanessa produced woodcuts for many of the early titles published by the Hogarth Press. One of the contentions between the sisters was children. Virginia was advised by her doctors not to have any children, and as such, was jealous of Vanessa's life with her children:

> 'I greatly envy your brats. They are very interesting. How odd it will be when Julian is a very clever, severe, undergraduate as I see he will be.'

Letter to Vanessa Bell, 30 July 1916

However, having children and working full time with her painting, made Virginia concerned about Vanessa's health too:

> '…Roger said you were overworked and was therefore doubtful about coming. I think it's most likely that you are overworked – and I do think it a most ridiculous thing, knowing what horror illness is… You use every

part of you, so incessantly.'

Letter to Vanessa Bell, 22 January 1917

Nessa married Clive Bell and had two children – Julian and Quentin. Throughout her personal writing, Virginia demonstrated a great deal of love for her nephews, often looking after them when Vanessa was ill or expecting her third child:

'Nevertheless to my thinking few people have a more vigorous grasp of a more direct pounce than Nessa. Two little boys with very active minds keep her in exercise…I suppose this is the effect of children and of responsibility, but I always remember it in her.'

Diaries, 2 November 1917

When Vanessa was expecting Angelica, her daughter by Duncan Grant, Virginia was thrilled at looking after the two boys:

'Of course we will have the children – there is nothing I should like better, and I will do my best not to let them come to grief in any way. If the baby doesn't arrive till after the 3rd you could send me a telegram and I would meet them at Victoria, and bring them here.'

Letter to Vanessa Bell, 12 December 1918

Still very excited to look after her nephews, Virginia describes what plans she has for them:

'I'm going to take them to the pantomime, and I've a great many plans for enjoying myself with them. I know I shall be more envious of you than ever when I get to know all their attractive ways – and of course they are the most adorable creatures. I find myself constantly thinking about them.'

Letter to Vanessa Bell, 17 December 1918

It seems thatVirginia was a doting and loving aunt:

'…and how Julian and Quentin were so much cleverer than most children.'

Diaries, 15 February 1919

Like most sisters, the relationship between Virginia and Vanessa did not always run smoothly. In an expressive diary entry in 1922, Virginia explains the disagreements that come between them:

'Nessa came again. How painful these meetings are! Let me try to analyse. Perhaps it is that we both feel that we can exist independently of the other. The door shuts between us, and life flows on again and completely removes the trace…

I set out to prove that being childless I was less normal than she. She took offence (the words are too strong). Told me I shouldn't enjoy café life in Paris. Told me I liked my own fireside and books and my friend's visits; implied that I was settled and unadventurous. Implied that I spent a great deal upon comfort. As we only had 2 hours together, and she left for Paris next morning, and perhaps I shan't see her till May, anyhow not continuously, I felt a sort of discontent, as the door closed behind her. My life, I suppose, did not very vigorously rush in.'

Diaries, 4 February 1922

Through her affair with Duncan Grant, Vanessa gained a daughter, Angelica. The relationship between Vanessa and her younger sister, Virginia, was one of fiercely protective love and intense rivalry. Together they survived their parents' deaths and other close family deaths in a short period of time. Described by Virginia as beautiful and '...also strong of brain, agile and determined.'[6] During the unhappy seven years between 1897 and 1904, Virginia describes her relationship with Vanessa as forming a close conspiracy and their own 'private nucleus'[7]. However, this was severely tested towards the end of 1906, beginning of 1907. As a member of the artistic circle of friends in Bloomsbury, Clive Bell had grown increasingly fond of Vanessa, and he first proposed to Vanessa in 1905. The following year, Clive asked her again and was rebuffed. However, when her brother Thoby Stephen became gravely ill with typhoid and passed away in November, Vanessa accepted Clive's marriage proposal just two days after Thoby's death. For Virginia, this seemed to be a double blow. Not only had she lost her brother (arguably her favourite), but now she was also losing Vanessa to Clive:

> '...there is, I think, something intellectual about him; something of the Cambridge standard, perhaps, surviving. He's no fool, though his manners suggest overwhelming reasons for thinking him one now and then – this perpetual effort to shine, to be 'in the know' – this vanity.'

> Diaries, 23 November 1917

> 'Clive has never forgiven me – for what? I see that he is carefully following a plan in his relations with me – and resents any attempt to distract him from it. His personal remarks always seem to be founded on some reserve of grievance, which he has decided not to state openly.'

> Diaries, 27 July 1918

In a letter to Violet Dickinson, a close friend of her half-sister Stella, on the day before Vanessa's wedding, Virginia writes: 'Really marriage makes very little difference – though I hate her going away.'[8] According to Jane Dunn, author of *Virginia Woolf and Vanessa Bell: A Very Close Conspiracy*, the competitiveness that lay between the sisters saw both trying to assert their own solidarities, and each had their own recognised territories: 'art versus literature, common sense versus sensibility, instinct versus intellectuality.'[9]

Throughout her life, whether directly or indirectly, Virginia maintained that her art of writing literature was superior to that of Vanessa's art of painting. On March 17th 1921, Virginia was in Manchester and visited an art gallery there. In a letter to Vanessa on the same day, she said 'Your art is far more of a joke than mine. But don't think I am unaware how dull this letter is.'[10]. Years later, in 1928, while writing to Vanessa's son Quentin, Virginia repeated her view that painting was a lesser art form: '…how in God's name can you be content to remain a painter? Surely you must see the infinite superiority of the language to the paint?'[11]. Virginia admitted to Duncan Grant that she was, in fact, jealous of Vanessa:[12]

'O but I've quarrelled with Nessa and Duncan! I'm standing on my dignity. They choose to tell me lies – very well, I don't go near them till I'm asked. Will they notice? Not in all that shindy of children &c: but I'm cheerful and composed, and conscious of the immense value of my visits.'

Diaries, 23 November 1920

The details of the above quarrel are unclear, but the Woolfs had purchased a cottage called Monk's House in Rodmell in 1919, and they were often near to Vanessa and

Duncan who had been living at Charleston in Sussex since 1916:

> 'Indeed, Nessa wouldn't have me living next door for something. Indeed, my retort is, I wouldn't live there. I see myself now taking my own line apart from theirs. One of these days I shan't know Clive if I meet him. I want to know all sorts of other people.'

Diaries, 19 December 1920

What is clear from the following quotation, is that Virginia is jealous of the emotional richness of Vanessa's life. She too has the desire for children, and can see how fulfilled Vanessa is by family life:

> 'We came back from Rodmell yesterday, and I am in one of my moods, as the nurses used to call it, today. And what is it and why? A desire for children, I suppose; for Nessa's life; for the sense of flowers breaking around me involuntarily. Here's Angelica – here's Quentin and Julian. Now children don't make yourself ill on plum pudding tonight. We have people dining. There's no hot water.'

Diaries, 2 January 1923

While discussing Quentin's future, Virginia once more raises her eyebrows at the art of the painter. Throughout her diaries, although she thinks Vanessa very talented, she disparages the art of painting:

> 'N and I sat talking, both now well-known women, if it comes to that. At dinner we discussed what school Quentin should go to. "He means to be a painter", said Nessa. "Yes" said Quentin, as if he were saying "yes, I am in love." At least it made me feel queer.'

Diaries, 13 June 1923

Virginia would often refer to Vanessa as being a genius, but this would always be said with a degree of jealousy.

Virginia's beloved brother, Thoby Stephen, had been a good friend of Clive Bell. Thoby had been an important figure in Virginia's childhood. He was a year and a half older than her, and she often confided in her big brother. In *Sketch of the Past*, she writes about how they argued over Shakespeare, and her belief that were it not for family tragedies, they would not have been as close. He is described as not being very clever, or funny, but rather clumsy and awkward[13]. She felt that he was naturally gifted, not silly like Adrian.

In 1906, the Stephens had decided that they wanted to visit Greece, and together with Violet Dickinson, an intimate friend of the family, they travelled there. While in Greece, Violet, Vanessa and Thoby all became seriously ill. On returning home, it transpired that Violet and Thoby were suffering from thyphoid. While Vanessa recovered from her illness, Thoby was diagnosed too late, and gradually became worse. On November 20th 1906, Thoby died from his fever, but Virginia was warned that if Violet found out about his death, then it could be fatal for her too, so the news had to be kept from her at all costs. Thus, Virginia wrote to Violet daily for weeks, giving her updates on Thoby's condition, even though he had already passed away. For example, on December 5th, she writes to Violet that 'Thoby goes on slowly… He likes being read to…'[14]. Ultimately, Violet discovered the truth when she read about Thoby's death in the *National Review*.

Adrian Stephen, born in 1883, seemed to have a curious relationship with Virginia. Analysing her diary and letters, she seems contemptuous of him. No letters from Virginia to Adrian survive. Unlike her other siblings, no full portrait of Adrian was made. Looking through her letters and diaries,

Virginia tends to be negative and critical of Adrian; as an example, in June 1919, she describes Adrian and his wife as a 'strange couple'[15]. This feeling was not helped when he married Karin Costelloe, who was disliked by the Woolfs:

> 'I wish he hadn't married her (you put this straight in the locked drawer, if not the w.c don't you?)…I think it's absurd to call Adrian a bore; he has great distinction; not that I could ever live with him tolerably…'

> Letter to Vanessa Bell, 15 July 1918

Virginia was not very kind when it came to describing Adrian's wife either, here comparing her to a dog, albeit a dog she grew very fond of:

> 'Karin came to give her lecture. I can't help being reminded by her of one of our lost dogs – Tinker most of all. She fairly races round a room, snuffs the corners of the chairs and tables, wags her tail as hard as she can.'

> Diaries, 5 February 1918

Although she might not have approved of his life choices, Virginia described Adrian as an intellectual, when he came to speak to the Women's Co-operative Guild in Richmond:

> 'Adrian and Karin dined here last night, and he spoke to the Guild on Peace – very composed, clear, well spoken, putting on his spectacles and reading in his pleasant intellectual voice from notes.

> He has traces of the judicial mind and manner.'

> Diaries, 10 July 1918

It wasn't just Virginia who was disparaging of her younger brother, but it seems that Vanessa, too, was not particularly fond of Adrian:

> 'Then we discussed the A.S's: he a dead weight, and she a live one, according to N who warns me we shall repent of asking them here this in front of Duncan too, who said nothing to contradict.'

Diaries, 16 August 1918

On getting to know the couple better, Virginia comes to realise why Karin is good for Adrian but the following comments show her disparagement of them and their children:

> 'Still, I do see why Adrian married her. First and foremost she makes him like other people. He has always, I believe, a kind of suspicion that whereas other people are professional, he remains an amateur. She provides him with household, children, bills, daily life, so that to all appearances he is just like other people.'

Diaries, 27 August 1918

> 'I've a new niece, Judith, not welcomed, but made the best of.'

Diaries, 30 November 1918

> 'Nessa comes back on Friday. Clive and Mary are in Paris. Then, I had tea with A and K on Sunday and saw all the children – Judith a great lump of a child; Ann with a look of the Watts' drawing of mother; yet both a good deal like Costelloes.'

Diaries, 11 May 1920

'I saw Adrian and Karin too. There's an unhappy

woman if you like. But what is happiness? I define it to be a glow in the eye. Her eyes are like polished pavements – wet pavements. There's no firelit cavern within.'

Diaries, 12 January 1924

Adrian received psychoanalytical treatment, and then decided to train as a psychoanalyst. Virginia's diary entry in 1923 reads: 'I am probably responsible. I should have paired with him, instead of hanging on to the elders.'[16]

Commenting upon his new career choice, Virginia admits that she is pleased for her brother.

'And Adrian is so happy and genial that I am really pleased. I don't want to make him out a failure even. An unambitious man, with good brains, money, wife and children is, I daresay, the most fortunate of us all. He need not protect himself by any illusions.'

Diaries, 14 February 1922

Adrian received psychoanalysis, and according to his wife, it left him broken but Virginia attests his fragility to his childhood:

'So he wilted, pale, under a stone of vivacious brothers and sisters…Ann is like him, pale, lank, sensitive, with the long, cold fingers I know so well…I liked Karin; pitied her too; and then felt come over me some mood of depression, not worth entering upon here.'

Diaries, 12 May 1923

Through her parents' earlier marriages, Virginia had other half siblings too. Laura Stephen (1870-1945) was the daughter of Leslie Stephen and Harriet Thackeray, but was considered psychotic, and was institutionalised.

In *Old Bloomsbury*, Virginia writes unkindly about Laura: '...a vacant-eyed girl whose idiocy was becoming daily more obvious.'[17] However, Laura lived to the age of 74 and died in 1945. In a letter to Vanessa in 1921, Virginia writes about having to pay for the cost of Laura's care:

> 'Laura's expenses are now £100 a year above her income. The trustees therefore say that we must somehow make this good. We owe her £2,000. There is however a sinking fund; in which they have invested some of her money every year, with a view to realising a capital sum in the year 1940. They propose that we should either mortgage this, or find £100 a year between us.'

Letter to Vanessa Bell, 24 October 1921

It is hard to know what Virginia felt about having a half-sister permanently locked away in an institution, but she may well have been afraid that she too could end up like Laura, both incurable and a financial burden on her family.

The Duckworth siblings on her mother's side, George, Stella and Gerald, each had vastly different effects on Virginia throughout her life. George (1868-1934), became a private secretary after his education, but in connection with Virginia, he is most associated with her early life. In *22 Hyde Park Gate*, included in *Moments of Being*, Virginia describes George as the family member who sexually abused her, painting him as 'not only father and mother, brother and sister to those poor Stephen girls; he was their lover also.' Vividly, Virginia describes the moment when George enters her room, tells her not to be scared and flings himself upon her. This was not the first and only time, but George would excuse his behaviour as comforting her in the light of her father's death. In *Sketch of the Past*, Virginia writes about her fear, shame and feeling of condemnation while George

112

analyses her appearance. However, George was not the only half-brother to abuse young Virginia. She writes honestly in *Sketch of the Past* about when Gerald, George's brother, took her onto his lap and 'explored' her body, touching her private parts. Gerald (1870-1937), founded the publishing house Duckworth & Co., and by 1913 had published various writers, including Henry James. In fact, Duckworth initially published Virginia's second novel, *Night and Day*, but then she bought back the rights to her first two novels:

> 'Yesterday I took *Night and Day* up to Gerald and had a little half domestic half professional interview with him in his office. I don't like the Club man's view of literature. For one thing it breeds in me a violent desire to boast: I boasted of Nessa and Clive and Leonard; and how much money they made.'

> Diaries, 2 April 1919

Stella (1869-1897), on the other hand, was a positive figure in Virginia's childhood, especially after their mother died. Treated severely by their mother, Stella took over the motherly duties when Julia died. Virginia writes fondly of Stella, mentioning her devotion to their mother and being reminded of a white flower whenever she thought of Stella. Stella's happiness grew when she became engaged and then married Jack Hills. However, this was to be short-lived, as Stella died soon after returning from honeymoon in July 1897. To add to the distress of her passing, it was discovered that Stella had been pregnant at the time of her death.

Other members of Virginia's extended family are also mentioned during the Richmond era. Sarah Emily Duckworth, affectionately known as Aunt Minna, was the sister of Julia Stephen's first husband. She lived most of her life in Hyde Park Gate until her death at the age of 90.

'I hear about once a month from Aunt Minna. She is generally under the impression that we're coming to stay with her for the weekend. Why should she ever die? It seems to me that no Duckworth need ever give way.'

Letter to Violet Dickinson, 14 January 1918

Upon hearing of Aunt Minna's death, Virginia wrote of her life:

'She merely lived all that length of time, without adventures, sorrows, difficulties, doubts, actions. She was always unperturbed. I think her great quality was her good sense. She was never in any way absurd or tiresome, & if necessary she would have been a person to ask some sorts of advice from.'[18]

Harry Stephen was one of Virginia's cousins. His father, James Fitzjames, was Leslie Stephen's brother. Harry went on to marry a niece of Florence Nightingale and had a son, who was later certified insane:

'A letter from Harry Stephen, suggesting a visit, as if he'd been in the habit of dropping in after dinner once a week all these years. The ties of blood? Something very odd moves in the Stephen brain.'

Diaries, 7 May 1918

'Mention of King George recalls Harry Stephen who sat like a frog with his legs akimbo, opening and shutting his large knife, and asserting with an egoism proper to all Stephens, that he knew how to behave himself, and how other people ought to behave.'

Diaries, 21 November 1918

Although she was different from Adrian, and as much as

she envied Vanessa, Virginia still thought of her family as a collective group of 'The Stephens':

> 'We Stephens, yes, and even Clive, with all his faults, had the initiative, and the vitality to conceive and carry our wishes into effect because we wished too strongly to be chilled by ridicule or checked by difficulty.'

Diaries, 24 January 1919

It seems that Virginia had issues with some members of her family as well as having her favourites. The relationships between family members were not always straightforward. However, she did keep in touch with various family members, either by writing letters to them or through family gatherings. She saw herself as belonging to a large clan of the Stephen family and always enjoyed receiving praise from them about her writing, especially from her sister Vanessa:

> 'Last night I dined for the first time with Clive in his rooms. Now I must make up my work account, for I have no time to say how strange that dinner was with Nessa and Clive again as we used to be so often; now a little formal superficially, and yet, miraculously, still intimate beneath: all 40 and over; all prosperous; and my book (that I felt somehow pleasing) acclaimed by Nessa "certainly a work of genius".'

Diaries, 7 November 1922

Virginia and her Servants

No one could be nicer than Nelly, for long stretches.

Diaries, 28 November 1919

From the time of Virginia's birth in 1882 at her home in 22 Hyde Park Gate, she was surrounded not only by her family but also by numerous servants. As noted in Alison Light's book *Mrs Woolf and the Servants*[1], Virginia had been '…kept clean, fed and watered by them [servants] ever since the nursery. She woke to find the curtains drawn and jugs of water placed beside her wash-basin; her clothes – mended, laundered, brushed – were laid out for her'. This was the kind of life that Virginia was accustomed to. Sophie, or Sophia, Farrell, probably the first major servant in Virginia's life, was the family cook from around 1886. She remained with the family, whether with the Stephens, Bells or Duckworths, for the rest of her working life. It seems that Virginia was fond of Sophie, as she was still in contact with her until at least 1939, when she is mentioned in a letter to Angelica Bell:

'Nessa might like to see this from old Sophie.'

Letter to Angelica Bell, 2 January 1939

According to the author Alison Light, Virginia and Sophie kept up a correspondence and Virginia sent Sophie an annual pension of £10 after she retired in the 1930s[2]. This clearly demonstrates that Virginia held her servants in high regard. In fact, in *Sketch of the Past*, while she was reminiscing about Stella Duckworth:

> 'Perhaps thus I think of her [Stella] less disconnectedly and more truly than anyone now living, save for Vanessa and Adrian; and perhaps old Sophie Farrell.[3]'

This was written in June 1939, and it is interesting that Virginia mentions Sophie in the same sentence as her two closest relatives, her surviving siblings, Vanessa and Adrian. It is quite possible that Sophie is mentioned as it is probable that she knew Stella in Virginia's early years. Even when the couple moved into the house of Mrs le Grys on Richmond Green, Virginia would recall how Sophie kept the house respectable, 'I believe that being curtained is a mark of respectability – Sophie used to insist upon it.'[4] As a lifelong and loyal family servant, Sophie remained in Virginia's mind, but this might not be said about the servants that were to enter the writer's life later.

Virginia often wrote about the servants she had with her at Hogarth House. The two main servants were Nellie (Nelly) Boxall and Lottie (Lotty) Hope; lifelong friends who, according to Virginia's diaries and letters, were often quick tempered. They came to the Woolfs from Roger Fry early in 1916:

> 'I do think Richmond has great charms also, and now we have Roger's servants, we keep clean.'

Letter to Katherine Cox, 12 February 1916

Sophie, by this time, was with the Duckworth side of the family, and came to visit Hogarth House soon after Nellie and Lottie arrived, and Virginia recorded preparations in a letter to her sister, Vanessa. According to the letter, Virginia told Nellie only good things about Sophie, but that her new servants had gone to tea with Vanessa's servant and had gossiped about Sophie. The letter continues:

> 'Nelly is an odd character – she sits up every night till 1 watching for zeppelins, and so I said she had better sleep in the kitchen, as a joke. But she took it up very seriously and is going to force Lottie to sleep with her in camp beds, among all the beetles.'

Letter to Vanessa Bell, 5 April 1916

By 1916, the First World War had been in progress for two years, and it was quite clear that the servants were worried about the bombing raids which had begun the previous year. Both the servants often slept in the kitchen, where occasionally Virginia and Leonard would join them. The sound of exploding bombs over central London probably forced them into the kitchen at the bottom of the house:

> '…by night we have the Aurora Borealis, which a man in the street took to be zeppelins… At midnight we heard them carrying their bedding to the kitchen, there to lie on the floor till day – With great difficulty we got them up again and lectured them on the nature of northern lights.'

Letter to Vanessa Bell, 22 January 1917

It seems that Virginia was concerned for the servants' comfort and welfare, not wanting them to spend the night on the kitchen floor, unnecessarily. Her desire to educate them extended to the subject of venereal diseases, following a lecture at the Women's Co-operative Guild:

> 'I spoke to Nelly (the cook) afterwards, and after being a little shocked, she agreed that it was most important that women should have knowledge in such matters [about the Guild lecture on venereal diseases]'

Letter to Margaret Llewelyn Davies, 26 January 1917

What follows in the letter is that Nellie and Virginia continued to talk about this, with the cook recounting tales of friends and family who had been affected. In fact, it was only through the servants that Virginia found out about the objections that some of the Guild members had about the lecture. Like many upper class women at the time, Virginia gained useful information from her servants.

One such example of this fairly unpredictable relationship is in 1917 during discussions about the time spent at Asheham House which was a country house in Sussex shared by Virginia and Vanessa:

> 'Nelly gave notice our last day at Asheham – as I expected. Neither she nor Lotty feel they can face 6 weeks there in the summer; so I'm speculating on a complete change – one servant, and meals from the communal kitchen.'

Letter to Vanessa Bell, 26 April 1917

This was to begin a few months of uncertainty in the domestic household, just as the couple had received their printing press. Generally, Virginia wrote to Vanessa with such domestic troubles, especially seeing as they would often lend and borrow each other's servants. After Nellie's resignation, Virginia was then determined to find a new servant to replace both Nellie and Lottie:

> 'The worst of it is that our domestics seem determined at last to settle in for ever; but our books are so high, and the difficulty of Asheham so great that I think I must change.'

Letter to Vanessa Bell, 27 June 1917

According to this letter, it was not just the fact that the servants did not wish to go to Asheham House, but also because money was tight with the expenses for the beginnings of the Hogarth Press. It seems that Virginia does not really want to change servants, but must due to circumstance. However, the predicament gets deeper:

'I have had a long talk with Nelly, and she agrees that they will never like Asheham, and so had better go. I then told her about Mary: and drew the most inviting picture I could of the place, but she said she did not wish to go there.'

Letter to Vanessa Bell, 3 July 1917

In this letter to Vanessa, Virginia has been trying to convince Nellie to go to another place of work, but the servant appears reluctant to do so. Later that same week, Virginia sends another letter to Vanessa, claiming that Lottie had come to see her to say that the pair would go to Asheham House after all. After making an offer to the pair, Lottie feels that it is probably best to make the break now:

'The worst of it is that Lottie [would] evidently stay on and like Asheham, if it weren't for Nelly and it seems a pity to lose her – but Nelly makes things too difficult with her boredom at Asheham.'

Letter to Vanessa Bell, 6 July 1917

This incident finally comes to a head later in the month, with Virginia writing that she had taken on the servants of Mary Hutchinson; Ethel and a cook.[5] It eventually turned out that the cook sent Virginia a letter saying she would not come because the work was in a basement, and so Virginia decided to ask Nellie and Lottie to stay:

'I think it is probable that Mary H. offered the cook a rise, and persuaded her to stay on; anyhow, I'm thankful, as it's much nicer to keep Lottie and Nelly, and they have made up their minds to put up with Asheham.'

Letter to Vanessa Bell, 26 July 1917

From this, it is clear that there was already a bond between mistress and servants, even if Nellie was not keen on going to Asheham House, probably due to its isolated, rural location, several miles from Lewes in Sussex. Hogarth House was certainly keeping the four inhabitants together. Even when Vanessa was having trouble with her servants, it was Nellie who looked for help among her friends and gave advice:

> 'Meanwhile Nelly is routing about among her friends and the servants where they are. She strongly advises you to advertise in the *West Sussex Gazette*, which one can get at Lewes.'

Letter to Vanessa Bell, 20 October 1917

At this point, the war was still raging, and this of course, would affect everyone in the country. Virginia showed her sympathetic side when Nellie's sister Liz was in need of some help:

> 'We are plunged in (temporary) difficulties: Liz has at last had her baby and her husband has been wounded at the same time, so that Nelly has had to go and look after her – however, I suppose we shall manage alright.'

Letter to Vanessa Bell, 22 October 1917

This event was important enough to grace Virginia's diary as well, but here she added on something extra that she did not say to her sister:

> 'Bert is wounded, and Nellie has gone to Liz. She felt it her duty and also her right – which shows how the

servant is bettering her state in this generation.'

Diaries, 22 October 1917

Here, in her private and personal writing, Virginia shows some respect for the servant who waits on her daily. It was clear that Virginia had a soft spot for both of her servants, notwithstanding some of the troubles she had with them:

'Nelly has just come back: the usual laughter begins again. We gave Lottie 5/ for doing so well.'

26 October 1917

As has been seen already, life with Nellie and Lottie could be extremely unpredictable, and only a few months later:

'This morning ruined by the tears and plaints of Lottie, who thinks her work too hard, and finally demanded higher wages, which she could easily get, and so could Nell. I lost my temper and told her to get them then. Up came Nelly in a conciliatory mood regretting Lottie's outburst; though pointing out the hardships of our printing-room, so untidy – work endless; had meant to ask a rise in February – everyone's wages raised…We were very amicable; no difficulty about money.'

Diaries, 12 December 1917

It seemed that the beginnings of the Hogarth Press were not only taxing for Leonard and Virginia, but also for Lottie and Nellie. Having a printing press in the house must certainly have been lots of extra work for the servants who had to clean it. This particular incident, however, was short-lived:

'By careful arrangement I limited the reconciliation scene with Lottie to 15 minutes at eleven sharp. She sobbed; repented; took back everything she'd said; told me how her temper had led to constant rows at Frys, as they call it…she begged me not to tell anyone; she kissed me and went off.'

Diaries, 13 December 1917

The 'Frys' that Lottie refers to must certainly be Roger Fry, from whom the pair of servants came. After this, domestic life seemed to settle down for the moment at least.

On January 25th 1918, it was Virginia's 36th birthday and:

> 'Nelly has knitted me a pair of red socks which tie around the ankle, and thus just suit my state in the morning. Another event kept me recumbent.'

Diaries, 25 January 1918

Virginia saw the irony in the colour of the socks with the onset of her menstruation. However, just four days later, the effects of the war would come very close indeed.

On Tuesday, January 29th 1918, two Kaiser war planes flew over London. One of them targeted the water works near Kew Bridge, now home to the London Museum of Water and Steam. A fourth bomb from the same plane targeted Kew station which flooded the tracks. Virginia records this event in her diary on the same day, detailing how they moved mattresses into the kitchen for safety:

> 'Servants became plaintive, and Lottie began talking of the effect upon her head; they hint that we ought to leave London.'

Diaries, 29 January 1918

In a letter to Vanessa with the same date, but finished two days later, Virginia writes; 'Well, you almost lost me.'[6]

The stress of the bombing raids must have had an effect on the servants too, making it hard for them to continue their domestic work:

> 'On Wednesday Lottie spilt half a case of type on the

floor, so that I had to spend 4 hours in sorting every compartment – about the most trying work there is. She had mixed the letters in thoroughly, thinking or hoping that though divided in compartments the letters were all the same.'

Diaries, 26 April 1918

In June 1918, Virginia still had money worries, and confided in Vanessa that the couple did not have enough money to keep the servants on. It seems that there had been an agreement with Vanessa for Lottie and Nellie to go to her to help her while she was pregnant, but on the proviso that the Woolfs could take them back at a later date if necessary. Virginia continues:

'Personally I think they're such good servants that some risk is worth running on your part – but it's all very complicated, and you're not in the least bound to have them in July.'

Letter to Vanessa Bell, 13 June 1918

'The question was whether N[ellie] and L[ottie] should go to Nessa for 3 months. At first they agreed with gladness; then they hesitated; then they asked for assurance that we would have them back.'

Diaries, 24 June 1918

This event was particularly complicated and could have easily created an argument between Virginia and Vanessa. There are numerous long letters from Virginia to her sister trying to explain the situation, whether Nellie and Lottie actually wanted to go, and if the Woolfs would take them back – it seems there was also confusion about the proviso that the Woolfs could get their servants back. Eventually:

'The servants want to stay on with us, but I've told them that we must discuss it later when we know for certain whether Leonard is going to get this editorship or not. We may hear next month.'

Letter to Vanessa Bell, 25 June 1918

The matter is complicated further when Nellie offers to go down to help Vanessa for two weeks, and this may have been offered by Nellie with an awareness that money was tight in the Woolf household that month and that wages might go unpaid.

The end of the war was coming, and on November 11th 1918, it officially ended - it was Armistice Day. Virginia's diary entry and letter to her sister were mostly concerned with this momentous event, but in the letter, she refers to how the servants were affected by the end of the war:

'How am I to write my last chapter with all this shindy, and Nelly and Lottie bursting in to ask – here is Nelly with 4 different flags which she is putting in all the front rooms. Lottie says we ought to do something, and I see she is going to burst into tears.'

Letter to Vanessa Bell, 11 November 1918

The last chapter to which Virginia refers, is the final chapter for *Night and Day*, which she finished ten days after Armistice Day.

About a month later, on Christmas Day 1918, Angelica Bell was born to Vanessa and her biological father, Duncan Grant. This event filled Virginia with much joy; so much so that Virginia wrote to Vanessa with a list of possible baby names. A month or so after this, Angelica became quite ill, and this resulted in the old question of whether Nellie and Lottie should go and help Vanessa:

'Nelly and Lottie would love helping to look after it...
Nelly's been extraordinarily nice, and says she would
do anything to help you, so do make any use of her
you can. I've just raised their wages, and they're both
overflowing with good will.'

Letter to Vanessa Bell, 1 February 1919

Nellie did in fact go to Vanessa, but Virginia insisted that
she be aided by another servant, and she found one by the
name of Phoebe Crane. However, there were problems with
Miss Crane, and she became ill. Eventually, she was well
enough to join Vanessa and Nellie returned to Richmond.
Vanessa had a very positive effect on Nellie:

'Nelly has come back in the highest spirits having
enjoyed herself immensely. In fact I see that I ought
to have made a condition that you shouldn't seduce
her by your charms.'

Letter to Vanessa Bell, 16 February 1919

Virginia also reveals that Nellie had told her that Vanessa
was not fond of Phoebe Crane, as she wouldn't do anything
beyond what she was paid to do. This led Virginia to suggest
finding a replacement. Moreover, Nellie had offered to go
down and help Vanessa whenever she was needed:

'You've made a complete conquest of Nelly; "such a
taking way with her", she says; and we're the nicest
pair of ladies she's ever known.'

Letter to Vanessa Bell, 18 February 1919

It transpires that Vanessa writes Nellie a letter (the
contents of which are not divulged), but this resulted in
considerable talk between the servant and Virginia. Nellie
would be willing to go back to Vanessa, but for Lottie, this
would lead to loneliness and much more hard work:

'She feels that she ought to go to you because you want her so much and she likes you so much; but if so Lottie must come too, and as this would be unfair to us, they would leave us and go to you permanently.'

Letter to Vanessa Bell, 24 February 1919

It was the same question all over again – whether the servants should stay with the Woolfs or move on. The situation culminated in a letter from Duncan Grant:

'Among my letters was one from Duncan, which looked to me ominous, and proved of course to contain a demand for Nelly as soon as possible... So I have wired to say she will go if possible for 3 weeks.'

Diaries, 15 March 1919

Nellie was sent to help Vanessa at Charleston for three weeks. Upon her return, things seemed to get back to normal, but by November, Nellie had grown tired of the constant dinner parties as well as having to look after Angelica:

'It was the dinner parties that led Nelly to give notice last Monday. She did it in a tentative boastful way, as if to show off to someone behind the scenes which makes me think she would be glad now to change her mind. She would this moment if I asked her.'

Diaries, 28 November 1919

Indeed, after this entry, there seems to be no more on the matter, until an entry towards the beginning of December. Apparently, Nellie had decided to stay:

'I stayed talking with Nelly when the rest were gone – about adders, about servants, George Eliot, & *Night & Day*.'

VIRGINIA WOOLF IN RICHMOND

Diaries, 6 December 1919

After spending some time at Rodmell, it appeared that Nellie had contracted whatever illness the Woolfs had had at Christmas:

> 'Didn't I come home to find that Nelly had declared herself dying, sent for another doctor and had entirely ruined poor L's evening. She's still in bed, seemingly ill as we were at Xmas; only now cheerful and sensible, and possibly to go home tomorrow.'

Diaries, 23 June 1920

Unfortunately, once back in Richmond, the situation had not got any better:

> 'Oh the servants! Oh reviewing! Oh the weather! …
> Nelly has vacillated between tears and laughter, life and death for the past 10 days; can't feel an ache anywhere without sending for me or L to assure her that aches are not certainly fatal. Then she cries.'

Diaries, 13 July 1920

Nellie soon recovered, and things returned to their usual routine. At least Virginia was happy with her domestic situation, even if Nellie was fearful of the printing press:

> 'Nelly panic struck, thinking it would come through the kitchen floor. How do you invent these fears? I asked her. Indeed, if she were so ingenious in her cooking we should do well… But never have we been so peaceful domestically for so long.'

Diaries, 16 November 1921

This domestic peace must have influenced the decision to increase the servants' wages just a few days later;

'Today we raise the servants' wages by £2 each; and Nelly, for a joke pretended that we had raised her and not Lottie, and I believe this has taken away Lottie's pleasure. I believe she suspects that we perhaps meant this, or preferred Nelly. At any rate, we have had no thanks.'

Diaries, 26 November 1921

Once again, in December, the household was struck down with disease; this time German measles. Instead of getting temporary replacements, Leonard and Virginia decided to do the housework themselves as no temporary replacement would come because of the risk of catching the disease:

'Alas! We're in the midst, or rather beginning, of a domestic crisis – both maids down with German measles, and no char will come for fear of infection, so Leonard carries the trays and I do the beds. I think anyhow I'd better not come, as at any moment we may break into rashes ourselves.'

Letter to Violet Dickinson, 10 December 1921

'Yes, I ought to be doing the beds; but Leonard insists upon doing them himself. Perhaps that's Lottie on the stairs? Ought I to go out and scold her for not staying in bed? Is the hot water on? … for 3 days we have been servants instead of masters.'

Diaries, 11 December 1921

One of the many things Virginia says about her servants is that they talk, and that they talk incessantly. If this had been a major problem for Virginia, she would not have kept them in the house for so long, so perhaps it is because she had formed a close, intimate bond with them that she allowed them to stay:

'Lottie's interminable gossip with the old witch wood woman frets me. Talk – talk – talk – wonder expressed loud laughter – agreement – wood woman's voice claps more and more emphatic – Nelly there too – Talk with them a kind of muscular activity I think, for they never say much.'

Diaries, 14 February 1922

'You can't question Nelly much without rubbing a sore. She threatens at once to send up a cheap meal "and Mr Woolf won't like that."'

Diaries, 18 February 1922

'Nelly and Lottie have talked till the sky seems nothing but a dish cover echoing their changes of mind. They go home for the week end to settle the matter, and eat birthday cakes, and I guess she won't go to hospital after all.'

Diaries, 24 March 1922

One of the bigger events to challenge Virginia during this period was the death of her friend and rival, Katherine Mansfield. It was Nellie who announced the news to Virginia:

'Nelly said in her sensational way at breakfast on Friday "Mrs Murry's dead! It says so in the paper!" At that one feels - what? A shock of relief? – a rival the less?'

Diaries, 7 January 1923

Time moved on, and it was decided that the Woolfs would move to Tavistock Square in central London. At the beginning of 1924, Virginia decided to break the news to her servants:

'On Saturday I deliver the sentence of death upon Nellie and Lottie; at Easter we leave Hogarth...Then Nelly presented her ultimatum - poor creature, she'll withdraw it, I know, - about the kitchen. "And I must have a new stove; and it must be on the floor so that we can warm our feet; and I must have a window in that wall..."... Such was our silent reflection as we recevied these commands, with Lottie skirmishing around with her own very unwise provisoes and excursions. "You won't get two girls to sleep in one room as we do" &c. "Mrs Bell says you can't get a drop of hot water in this house..." "So you won't come here again, Nelly?" I asked. "No ma'am, I won't come here again" in saying which she spoke, I think, the truth. Meanwhile, they are happy as turtles, in front of a roaring fire in their own clean kitchen, having attended the sales, and enjoyed all the cheap diversions of Richmond.'

Diaries, 3 January 1924

Virginia was determined not to leave Nellie and Lottie unemployed, and eventually the couple managed to persuade Nellie to stay with them in Tavistock Square, and Virginia would try to get Lottie to Gordon Square with Adrian and Karin Stephen, although Lottie declared she would be more than happy to go to Vanessa:

'... we have asked Nelly to stay on as general, which, greatly, to our relief, she has agreed to do. I then suggested that I should try to find Lottie a place in Gordon Sqre. She said at once that she would be perfectly happy if she could be with you.'

Letter to Vanessa Bell, 11 January 1924

In the same letter, Virginia wrote fondly and pleasantly

of Lottie, saying that her temper is not something to worry about and that she has such a nice character. This continues in Virginia's diary entry of the following day, but she is more candid about her worries:

'As for Lottie, I have my doubts, for her temper will always be unseating her, and I feel, after 7 years, or is it 8?, some responsibility for her. If by my doing she got into difficulty, I suppose I should blame myself.'

Diaries, 12 January 1924

Even with their resignations on a number of occasions, Nellie and Lottie remained dedicated to Virginia and Leonard throughout their time in Richmond, running the household and enabling the couple to focus on their work.

Nellie Boxall had come to work for the Woolfs in 1916, having worked for Roger Fry previously. She not only continued to work for Virginia and Leonard throughout the Richmond years, but joined them at Tavistock Square and Rodmell until 1934. After years of service, there was a quarrel between Nellie and Virginia, which is scrupulously described in her diary and letters to Ethel Smyth, and ultimately, Nellie was dismissed on March 27th 1934:

'In the intervals she was angelic and an admirable cook – and then 6 weeks ago today, when I was ill, there was a row over an electric oven, which we wanted to try, and she wouldn't.'

Letter to Ethel Smyth, 29 March 1934

It was therefore an argument over an oven which ultimately ended Nellie Boxall's eighteen years of service.

Lottie Hope came with Nellie from Roger Fry's house to the Woolfs in 1916, but when the move was made to Tavistock Square, Lottie did not go with them, but instead moved to Gordon Square with Adrian and Karin Stephen. She continued working for members of the extended family until 1941.

However, it seems that, even with faults and quarrels, Virginia was very fond of both of her servants. There's no doubt that Nellie and Lottie were important in providing a stable household at Hogarth House and carrying out the domestic duties which enabled Virginia and Leonard to have time for their work.

Gatherings with Woolf

And at this moment the mere length of my list of unrecorded visitors frights me from beginning.

Diaries, 18 April 1918

Even though Virginia might have felt alone during her illnesses and troubles, she certainly kept up with society, having numerous visitors come to Richmond to see her and Leonard. A lot of these gatherings were for lunch or dinner and sometimes to stay over for the night. Not including her family members, such as Vanessa and Clive Bell, and Adrian and Karin Stephen, most of the well-known names come from the original incarnation of the Bloomsbury Group. Included in some of the quotes below is John Maynard Keynes (1883-1946), a writer on economics, who had once shared a house with the Woolfs; the Hogarth Press also published three of his pamphlets.

> 'Maynard Keynes came to dinner. We gave him oysters. He is like quicksilver on a sloping board – a little inhuman, but very kindly, as inhuman people are.'

Diaries, 20 January 1915

Maynard Keynes was to remain in Virginia's life, and she would value his opinions – especially that of *The Years*.

> 'Maynard thinks *The Years* my best book… he thought

The Years very moving, more tender than any of my books.'

Diaries, 4 April 1937

Another member of the Bloomsbury Group was Lytton Strachey (1880-1932), a critic and biographer. Strachey had actually proposed to Virginia in February 1909, but this was quickly recanted as a mistake by both, and he encouraged Leonard to propose. Strachey remained a lifelong friend, and the Woolfs were devastated when he died in 1932. However, it was clear that Virginia cherished his friendship:

'Nothing is easier or more intimate than a talk with Lytton. If he is less witty, he is more humane.'

Diaries, 22 January 1919

Virginia found Lytton entertaining and could spend hours talking with him on a variety of subjects. One of the most interesting conversations took place in January 1918:

'Lytton came to tea; stayed to dinner, and about 10 o'clock we both had that feeling of parched lips and used up vivacity which comes from hours of talk. But Lytton was most easy and agreeable. Among other things he gave us an amazing account of the British Sex Society which meets at Hampstead.'

Diaries, 21 January 1918

In this diary entry, Virginia goes into much more detail about the kinds of topics which were discussed at the society, including incest, self-abuse and whether cats use the W.C. Virginia seemed so intrigued that she states, 'I think of becoming a member.'[1] One thing that Lytton and Virginia often talked about was writing:

'Lytton came to tea on Friday and half maliciously

assured me that my industry amazed him. My industry and my competence, for he thinks me the best reviewer alive, and the inventor of a new prose style, and the creator of a new version of the sentence.'

Diaries, 25 May 1919

Since Lytton was also a writer, the pair could talk about anything literary; Virginia encouraged him to write plays or stories, but this advice was not heeded. Virginia valued Lytton's criticism on her own work, notably when she had finished *Mrs Dalloway*, 'No, Lytton does not like *Mrs Dalloway* and, what is odd, I like him all the better for saying so and don't much mind… he says sometimes the writing is of extreme beauty.'[2] Whatever the topic, it seemed that Virginia and Lytton had a very understanding relationship:

'Lytton lunched here, and we examined his soul under the apple trees, and gave it back to him without serious criticism.'

Letter to Lady Ottoline Morrell, 21 May 1919

The relationship between the two writers was both intense and intimate:

'Lytton dined here the other night – a successful evening. Oh I was right to be in love with him 12 or 15 years ago. It is an exquisite symphony his nature when all the violins get playing as they did the other night; so deep, so fantastic.'

Diaries, 17 October 1924

When Lytton died in 1932, Virginia was heartbroken. In a similar manner to how she felt about Katherine Mansfield, Virginia writes to Dora Carrington:

'I find I can't write without suddenly thinking Oh but

Lytton won't read this, and it takes all the point out of it. I always put away things in my mind to say to Lytton.'

Letter to Dora Carrington, 31 January 1932

Dora Carrington (1893-1932), known by her surname alone, became a friend of the Woolfs during a stay at Asheham, their country house, in 1915. Carrington fell in love with Lytton Strachey and became his companion, but shortly after his death, she committed suicide. She often came with Lytton, and sometimes alone, to visit Virginia and Leonard:

'On Saturday the chatter began. Lytton and Carrington came to tea – she apple red and firm in the cheeks, bright green and yellow in the body, and immensely firm and large all over. The talk has run off my mind, so I don't suppose there was anything said of great importance.'

Diaries, 18 March 1918

Virginia very rarely had anything negative to say about Carrington, showing that she was very fond of her. In fact, after Lytton's death, Leonard and Virginia were some of the last people to see Carrington alive before she committed suicide by gunshot:

'Then Carrington came to tea with me, L making a speech again… Carrington stayed over 2 hours, and I think that by itself is a sign of youth. She is odd from her mixture of impulse and self-consciousness. I wonder sometimes what she's at: so eager to please, conciliatory, restless and active.'

Diaries, 6 June 1918

It was clear that Virginia enjoyed having company, even if Leonard would worry that she might over-exert herself. The list of visitors kept growing. Here are just two examples:

> 'On Sunday the burden of visitors was oppressive. The list speaks for itself. Gerald and Saxon lunch: Saxon tea; Barbara, Nick, Middleton Murry dinner. Gerald's likeness to a pampered overfed pug dog has much increased. His hair is white. There is hardly a gleam of life, let alone intelligence in his eye.'

Diaries, 18 March 1918

> 'And at this moment the mere length of my list of unrecorded visitors frights me from beginning. Judge Wadhams, Hamilton Holt, Harriet Weaver, Ka, Roger, Nessa, Maynard, Shepherd, Goldie, not to mention the Guild and Alix and Bryn and Noel, (who may be called the 17 Club) all these have accumulated since Sunday; and each deserves something to mark their place, and I did mark it at the time.'

Diaries, 18 April 1918

The novelist Edward Morgan Forster (1897-1970) was another Bloomsbury member, who published seven titles with the Hogarth Press, including *The Story of the Siren* in 1920. Virginia was very keen to receive Forster's reviews of her works, and almost looked upon him as a mentor. Virginia liked Forster, but found him to be rather restless:

> 'I like Forster very much, though I find him whimsical and vagulous to an extent that frightens me with my own clumsiness and definiteness.'

Diaries, 12 July 1919

Although Virginia found him whimsical, she also could

see that he had sensitvity and kindness. She mentions one time when she saw him:

> 'I saw Forster, who is as timid as a mouse, but when he creeps out of his hole very charming. He spends his time in rowing old ladies upon the river and is not able to get on with his novel.'

Letter to Margaret Llewelyn Davies, 31 August 1915

Upon receiving his review for *Night and Day*, in which he states that he liked it less than *The Voyage Out*, Virginia writes:

> 'Yet I suppose I value Morgan's opinion as much as anybodies.'

Diaries, 30 October 1919

In addition to this review, which was not the most favourable for Virginia, Forster would send reviews of nearly all of her work, and the letter she received about *Jacob's Room* was the letter she liked best of all.[3] However, soon after his review of *Night and Day* Forster would visit Virginia:

> 'Sydney and Morgan dined with us last night. On the whole, I'm glad I sacrificed a concert. The doubt about Morgan and [*Night and Day*] is removed; I understand why he likes it less than V.O and in understanding, see that it is not a criticism to discourage.'

Diaries, 6 November 1919

The Sydney referred to here is likely to be Sydney Waterlow, a British diplomat, who along with his wife Margery, were also part of Virginia's circle.

As well as having individuals and couples over to visit, reading through the diaries, there are many mentions of dinner parties held at the Woolfs' house:

> 'On Sunday, that is the 1st December we had a dinner party. Six people make a dinner party. They destroy private conversation. You have to be festive. We had Nick, Carrington, Mrs Manus and Sanger: and I think it was a successful party.'

Diaries, 3 December 1918

> 'We dine of course out of doors to the sound of the fountain. The robins douche themselves there. Last night there were six voices to drown its perpetual dripping.'

Diaries, 22 May 1919

Other Bloomsbury visitors included Desmond and Molly MacCarthy, and Saxon Sydney-Turner. Desmond MacCarthy was a well-known critic and journalist. He joined the *New Statesman*, initially as a drama critic and from 1917 as literary critic. He eventually worked for the *Sunday Times* as a literary critic. Molly MacCarthy was a writer and was instrumental within the Bloomsbury Group when she formed The Memoir Club.

Saxon Sydney-Turner was an intellectual with a love of poetry, and his conversations were welcomed in the Bloomsbury Group. He worked as a civil servant in the treasury department throughout his career.

Roger Fry, of whom Virginia wrote a biography after he died in 1934, was another frequent guest. Roger Fry (1866-1934) was a British painter and critic and was also to be a major figure in Virginia's life. Their relationship also consisted of talk of literature and painting; what Virginia thought of him when it was discovered that he was having a love affair with her sister, Vanessa, is uncertain.

Whatever she thought of his affair, she still admired him:

> 'Yesterday we talked from 1.30 to 7 without stopping.
> Roger appeared with Pamela and a Russian lady. Roger
> is a miracle.'

Letter to Vanessa Bell, 18 May 1919

Roger also seemed to be an encouraging voice to Virginia when she was doubting herself:

> 'And then there was Roger who thinks I'm on the track
> of real discoveries, and certainly not a fake.'

Diaries, 12 April 1921

In the same entry, Virginia describes Roger coming to the house again, working on his woodcuts. The Hogarth Press published *Twelve Original Woodcuts* by Roger Fry in December 1921. Unfortunately, in 1934, Roger Fry died of heart failure after a fall, and this was something of a shock to all those that knew him:

> 'I wish you had known him. He was so extraordinarily
> alive – I still find myself thinking I shall tell him
> something. And we all lived so much together. Dear
> me, why must one's friends die?'

Letter to Vita Sackville-West, 23 September 1934

Other notable names include writers such as Katherine Mansfield (1888-1923), a short story writer from New Zealand. Her work *Prelude* was published in 1918 by the Hogarth Press. She married John Middleton Murray in the same year, and both were guests of the Woolfs. Virginia's descriptions of Mansfield are not entirely positive:

> 'We could both wish that one's first impression of
> K.M. was not that she stinks like a – well civet cat

that had taken to street walking. In truth, I'm a little shocked by her commonness at first sight; lines so hard and cheap. However… she is so intelligent and inscrutable.'

Diaries, 11 October 1917

It seemed that Virginia was rather confused about Katherine, and did not know whether to class her as a friend due to the lack of written communication from her:

'It is at this moment extremely doubtful whether I have the right to class her among my friends. Quite possibly I shall never see her again. Upstairs I have letters in which she speaks of finding the thought of me a joy.'

Diaries, 18 February 1919

On the contrary to this, Virginia did indeed see Katherine again, and it was due to illness that Mansfield had not written.

After Mansfield's death in 1923, Virginia felt desolate because Katherine would never read her work again and she thought that they had had something in common:

'Yet I have the feeling that I shall think of her at intervals all through my life. Probably we had something in common which I shall never find in anyone else.'

Diaries, 16 January 1923

The American writer T.S. Eliot (1888-1965) was invited by Leonard to send some poems to the Press, and his collection of *Poems* was published in 1919, followed by *The Waste Land* in 1923:

'I was interrupted somewhere on this page by the

arrival of Mr Eliot... a polished, cultivated, elaborate young American, talking so slow, that each word seems to have special finish allotted it. But beneath the surface, it is fairly evident that he is very intellectual, intolerant, with strong views of his own.'

Diaries, 15 November 1918

Even though Virginia appeared to be unsure of Eliot at first, their friendship would only deepen over the years:

'We've been having that strange young man Eliot to dinner. His sentences take such an enormous time to spread themselves out that we didn't get very far.'

Letter to Roger Fry, 18 November 1918

'And the Eliots, Walter and Marjorie dined here on Sunday; I amused myself by seeing how sharp, narrow and much of a stick Eliot has come to be, since he took to disliking me. His wife awashed out, elderly and worn looking little woman.'

Diaries, 10 April 1919

Two years later, Virginia was still musing over what would happen with their friendship:

'What about Eliot? Will he become 'Tom'? What happens with friendships undertaken at the age of 40? Do they flourish and live long? I suppose a good mind endures, and one is drawn to it and sticks to it, owing to having a good mind myself. Not that Tom admires my writing, damn him.'

Diaries, 13 March 1921

One very interesting meeting with Eliot resulted in him reading *The Waste Land* to her, which she listened to with great enthusiasm:

> 'Now I have little time for anything else. We have seen a great many people. Roger's lectures provide a rendezvous. Eliot dined last Sunday and read his poem. He sang it and chanted it rhythmed it. It has great beauty and force of phrase: symmetry; and tensity.'

Diaries, 23 June 1922

Further still, Virginia still considers Eliot to be strange, but here there seems to be some pity for him:

> 'What gossip is there? That strange figure Eliot dined here last night. I feel that he has taken the veil, or whatever Monk's do. He is quite calm again. Mrs Eliot has almost died at times in the past month. Tom, though infinitely considerate, is also perfectly detached. His cell, is I'm sure, a very lofty one, but a little chilly. We have the oddest conversations: I can't help but loosing some figure of speech, which Tom pounces upon and utterly destroys. Never mind: I loose another. So we go on.'

Letter to Roger Fry, 18 May 1923

Eliot and the Woolfs remained close, and it has been suggested that he inspired the character of Louis in *The Waves*.

One of the people to whom Virginia wrote many letters is Margaret Llewelyn Davies (1861-1944), who was the general secretary of the Women's Cooperative Guild until 1921. She was also a suffragist who from 1904, led the Guild to be part of the non-militant campaign for the vote. Margaret's commitment to pacifism during the First World War, led to her election to the General Council of the Union of Democratic Control, which called for a negotiated peace.

She was also a social worker who campaigned for the rights of women, including a rise in the minimum wage.

Margaret seemed to be a confidante for Virginia, and they remained lifelong friends. Along with her companion, Lillian Harris, Margaret often came to visit Virginia and Leonard:

> 'I remember though that we walked, printed and Margaret came to tea. How pale these elderly women get! The rough pale skin of toads, unfortunately: M. in particular easily loses the flash of her beauty.'

> Diaries, 23 October 1917

> 'We had a visit from Margaret; which opened with a tremendous broadside of cooperative shop; lamentations, aspirations and too sanguine expectations; all exaggerated, so I felt, in comparison with their real value.'

> Diaries, 24 June 1918

Katherine (Ka) Arnold-Foster, née Cox (1887-1938) first met Virginia in 1911 and was nicknamed 'Bruin', or the bear. Ka was very important in Virginia's early life and was involved in helping Virginia when she became ill. Leonard asked her to come to the couple while they were on holiday to help bring Virginia back to London. It was also to Ka that Virginia made this very intimate remark after her honeymoon:

> 'Why do you think people make such a fuss about marriage and copulation? Why do some of our friends change upon losing chastity? Possibly my great age makes it less of a catastrophe; but certainly I find the climax immensely exaggerated.'

> Letter to Katherine Cox, 4 September 1912

Ka was a fairly regular visitor, where Virginia would write about her in her diary:

> 'The sweetness of Ka's nature, so we thought, is triumphing over the bureaucracy which threatened to straitwaistcoat all her charm... She complains of falling hair; but looked to me softer and rosier, and more of the smoothness of cream than for a long while.'

Diaries, 19 October 1917

However, even though Ka was to feature in the early part of Virginia's life, the two women would lose contact after Ka's marriage to Mark Arnold-Foster. In a letter to Virginia, Ka rightly assumed that Virginia would not approve of Mark, as quoted in Quentin Bell's biography of Virginia. During the First World War, Ka Cox had helped with the refugee effort in Corsica, and then later she became the first woman magistrate in Cornwall.

In all of the locations Virginia Woolf lived, she was inundated with a great many visitors. Mostly, these were invited by Virginia, even though she would often complain of the large numbers of people visiting. She wrote about the tireless conversations as well as scathing, but sometimes pleasant, descriptions of her visitors. Mainly through her diaries, one can discover Virginia's true feelings towards the people she surrounded herself with.

> 'But first let me recall Janet, Desmond, Katherine Mansfield and Lilian; there were others, - yes, there was Harry Stephen and Clive. Each left with me a page full of comments, but useless now partly I think from my habit of telling these incidents over to people, and once told, I don't want to retell them.'

Diaries, 25 May 1918

'Here is my calendar: Tuesday the Squires and Wilkinson and Edgar to dinner, Wednesday tea with Elena; Thursday lunch with Nessa, tea Gordon Square; Friday Clive and Mary here; and Saturday sitting over the fire with a morbid and I hope unfounded fear lest certain creatures infesting Lottie and Nelly may begin to twitter beneath my skin.'

Diaries, 31 January 1920

Although Virginia clearly enjoyed the company of a wide range of diverse personalities, it seemed that she would have liked to write about each one, but found that she didn't have the time:

'We see too many people for me to describe them, had I the time.'

Diaries, 23 November 1920

'I have seen quantities of people – having them here, as my invalid ways induced, bright pictures, tunes on the gramophone – but I must not insult the human soul for which I have really so much respect.'

Diaries, 28 January 1923

One of the most influential people in Virginia's life was Vita Sackville-West (1892-1962), who, along with her husband, Harold Nicolson, met the Woolfs in December 1922 at a dinner party hosted by Clive Bell. Virginia describes Vita as 'lovely, gifted aristocratic' and continues:

'Not much to my severer taste – florid, moustached, parakeet coloured, with all the supple ease of the aristocracy, but not the wit of the artist… But could I ever know her? I am to dine there on Tuesday.'

Diaries, 15 December 1922

There is very little account of the dinner Virginia had with Vita later in December 1922. At this point, Vita had just published *Knole and the Sackvilles*, a history of her family at their ancestral home, Knole, near Sevenoaks in Kent. The first letters between the women concerned Virginia receiving a copy of this book. Upon receiving it, and reading through it, Virginia wrote to Vita again:

> 'I should never have dared to dun you if I had known the magnificence of the book. Really, I am ashamed and would like to say that copies of all my books are at your service if you raise a finger.'

Letter to Vita Sackville-West, 3 January 1923

It seems that the two women were forming an already close bond, having only met the month before. There was flattery to-and-fro, in which both women praised the others' work. In the same letter, Virginia asks Vita to dine with them at Hogarth House. It seems fitting that their love affair, which lasted many years, possibly started in the town of Richmond. Vita dined with the couple on 11th January 1923, although according to Leonard, they did not see much of Vita for the rest of the year. However, in February, Vita and her husband visited the couple:

> 'We had a surprise visit from the Nicolsons. She is a pronounced Sapphist, and may, thinks Ethel Sands, have an eye on me, old though I am... Snob as I am, I trace her passions 500 years back, and they become romantic to me, like old yellow wine.'

Diaries, 19 February 1923

Their friendship grew stronger over the next few years, and The Hogarth Press published thirteen works by Vita. It is well-known that Virginia and Vita had an intense love affair, most likely at its height between 1925 and 1928, and this has been subject to much research and interest, including a play and a film written by Eileen Atkins. Perhaps the greatest gift that emerged from their love affair was *Orlando*, published in 1928 and dedicated to Vita. Reading like a love letter to Vita, Virginia describes how she took inspiration from her lover:

> 'Tomorrow I begin the chapter which describes Violet and you meeting on the ice. The whole thing has to be gone into thoroughly. I am swarming with ideas.'

Letter to Vita Sackville-West, 13 October 1927

However, at the time of *Orlando*'s publication, Vita was already having other affairs, and it was clear to Virginia that she could not satisfy Vita's needs. It is possible that *Orlando* was written as a farewell, even though the women kept in contact up until the time of Virginia's death.

Health

*Far from being brilliant, I spent most of the summer in bed
or on the verge of it, completely comatose. But then life is so
pleasant when one gets up again.*

Letter to Lady Ottoline Morrell, 8 November 1921

The health of Virginia Woolf has long been a topic of
interest for biographers and scholars. Some authors have
suggested that today, Virginia would be diagnosed as
suffering from bi-polar disorder. But in Edwardian times,
mental health issues were commonly referred to as 'trouble
with one's nerves'. It wasn't until the end of the First
World War that psychoanalytical societies were established
internationally. During the pre-war era, there was debate
over whether Freud's theories about the subconscious mind
were valid and rival theories were put forward by Jung and
Adler.

Virginia was not a fan of psychoanalysis, and was unhappy
when her half-brother Adrian underwent therapy, and then
studied in order to become a psychoanalyst. The Hogarth
Press helped to promote the psychoanalytic movement
when it published the twenty-four volumes of *The Standard
Edition of the Complete Psychological Works of Sigmund Freud*
(1953-1974), but before the First World War, understanding
of mental health was in its infancy. Treatments had
improved since the purging, bloodletting and cold baths
which were administered to patients in Victorian times.

Patients suffering from mental illness were often housed in large asylums where they could be strapped to chairs and medicated. They were given moral and religious instruction, and kept busy sewing, or carrying out menial work, to prevent them dwelling on their condition. Fresh air and exercise were considered necessary for recovery.

In *Beginning Again* and *Downhill All the Way*, two volumes of Leonard Woolf's autobiography, he outlines, in some detail, the mental breakdowns that Virginia suffered, describing the two stages of Virginia's madness – the manic and depressive. In the manic stage, she was reported to be very excited, talked incessantly and spoke of delusions and voices that she could hear. In the depressive stage, she was the complete opposite; very melancholic, did not want to speak and refused to eat – Leonard writes of having to try to force her to eat, even only small mouthfuls. Through these episodes, she lost an incredible amount of weight and the onset of her periods often led her to remaining 'recumbent' in bed, due to the 'usual circumstances'. It was also in this stage that she refused to believe she was ill, and it was this that led to her suicide attempts.

In the 1936 episode, Virginia was going through the proofs of *The Years* and Leonard states in *Downhill All the Way* that she 'was much nearer a complete breakdown than she had ever been since 1913.'[1] However, Leonard also states that he believed that Virginia's genius was connected to her madness.

In June 1910, Virginia was so ill that Vanessa came to the conclusion that she wouldn't be able to look after her. After all, she was heavily pregnant with her son Quentin. In communication with one of Virginia's doctors, Dr Savage, it was Vanessa who suggested that Virginia should enter a 'rest home'. In total, Virginia spent four periods at Burley House, which was a nursing home for women with nervous disorders, located at 15 Cambridge Park, Twickenham. As described by Quentin Bell, Burley was 'a polite madhouse for female lunatics'[2]. Miss Jean Thomas, proprietor of Burley, was the overseer there and after Virginia's first stay in 1910, Miss Thomas even accompanied her patient on a walking holiday in Cornwall in August and remained involved in Virginia's life for the next few years. Leonard did not seem convinced by Miss Thomas' involvement, stating that she was '…somewhat emotional and adored Virginia, a combination which had its disadvantages.'[3] Despite these disadvantages, Virginia returned to Burley House in February 1912, July 1913 and March 1915.

While incarcerated at Burley, there were many restrictions put on patients, which included being kept in a darkened room with very little access to letters, reading or visitors. Rest cures such as these were commonplace in those times. Often, patients were fed a milk diet, or in some cases overfed milk, before moving on to meat. Fresh air was also prescribed as well as the possibility of excitement being severely limited. Patients were instructed to be taken away from the home with no communication with their family[4]. In her biography, Hermione Lee states that Woolf was prescribed many different sedatives, and questions what the effects of the illness were in comparison with the effects of the treatment.[5] In one of the more shocking treatments, it was thought that pulling teeth was a cure for madness, due to the removal of bacteria beneath the root of the tooth. As a result of this, Virginia had teeth removed in 1919 as well as 1922.

During these episodes of mental illness, Virginia generally avoided writing in her diary; mainly because this was discouraged at Burley. However, just before her entry to the home in 1910, she wrote to her sister, Vanessa. In the letter dated Friday June 24th 1910, she expresses disappointment at Dr Savage's decision and is 'rather cross' that he didn't push for her to go to Burley immediately. Virginia does not look forward to going to the home, but states 'I also imagine the delights of being sane again'[6]. However, her language in the next letter to Vanessa is much stronger and filled with disdain as she writes from the home. Dated July 28th 1910, she begins with 'Beloved, or rather, Dark Devil' when addressing her sister. Written fairly coherently, she lashes out at Vanessa ('I want intelligent conversation – even yours) and her unborn child ('deformities'), convinced there is a conspiracy against her. Even through these veiled insults, Woolf manages to write with much beauty; 'I feel my brains, like a pear, to see if it's ripe; it will be exquisite by September'.

In 1912, Virginia had already been introduced to Leonard Woolf, and they had formed a friendly relationship. In January of the same year, Leonard asked Virginia to marry him. Virginia certainly liked him, but she hadn't prepared an answer for him, and wanted to get to know him better. Leonard wrote to her a few times in that month, but by that time, Virginia had lapsed into ill health once again, and in February, Virginia returned to Burley House for two weeks, according to her letter to Lytton Strachey dated February 16th 1912.

There had been an earlier marriage proposal from Lytton Strachey, which was withdrawn, and it was with considerable insight that Lytton suggested that Leonard Woolf might prove a good match. Virginia and Leonard found a bond over literature and politics. Leonard's calm nature and the skills gained in his post in the Ceylon Civil Service, provided a good counter-balance to Virginia's impulsivity and restlessness. They were married in August 1912, and in *Beginning Again*, Leonard writes that he had no clear knowledge or understanding of the fragility of

Virginia's health[7]. However, on March 5th 1912, Virginia wrote Leonard a letter in which she states:

> 'I shall tell you wonderful stories of the lunatics. By the bye, they've elected me King. There can be no doubt about it.'

Letter to Leonard Woolf, 5 March 1912

1913, according to biographers such as Hermione Lee and Leonard Woolf himself, was seen to be the start of the worst period of mental instability for Virginia. At the beginning of this period, Virginia was finishing *The Voyage Out*, which she appeared to have a great deal of trouble completing. Leonard claims that she rewrote the final chapters of the book many times over. The fear that Virginia had was that her book would be rejected and jeered at by critics, and this feeling continued throughout the first six months of 1913. In July, however, Leonard consulted doctors and was advised that Virginia should return to Burley, and indeed she stayed there from July 25th to August 11th. Virginia refers to this incident years later in 1936, while working on final editions of *The Years*, where in a diary entry, she states that she has '...never been so near the precipice to my own feeling since 1913'[8]. During her few weeks back at Burley, Virginia spent most of her time resting and eating, occasionally reading magazines. There are few letters from this time to Leonard, but when they are written, they are full of remorse for causing all this trouble, as well as professions of love.

After her stay at Burley, Leonard took Virginia to Somerset in the hope that the change of scenery might help her to recover. Unfortunately, the holiday proved a mistake and Virginia became even more depressed. Clearly feeling out of his depth, Leonard sent for Virginia's close friend Ka Cox to join them in Somerset. It was decided that they should return to London for more consultations with medical professionals, and they returned to London on August 22nd. However, Virginia's depression became chronic, and around September 10th, Leonard received a telephone message from Ka Cox informing him that she had discovered Virginia unconscious from taking an overdose of veronal, a type of barbiturate. She was rushed to a hospital where her stomach was pumped and did not regain consciousness until two days later. In *Beginning Again*, Leonard takes full responsibility for this, as he usually kept his case which contained the drug locked, but on that day, it appears he left it open and Virginia found the unlocked case:

> 'I want just to tell you how wonderfully things have changed in the last few days. I am now all right though rather tired. It is so wonderful that I can hardly believe it.'

Letter to Margaret Llewelyn Davies, 25 February 1915

According to Leonard, who had to adapt to becoming Virginia's full-time carer, her bouts of mental instability continued, albeit sporadically, into 1915. Towards the end of 1914, on Leonard's insistence, the couple moved into rooms at 17, The Green, in Richmond and early the following year, Leonard had secured a lease for Hogarth House and the couple were due to move in during March. However, the stress of moving as well as the forthcoming publication of her debut novel, may have contributed to Virginia's anxiety becoming heightened and she relapsed, becoming incoherent and talking gibberish before lapsing into a coma. Not wanting to impose the burden of dealing with this illness on their landlady, Mrs le Grys, Leonard was keen to prepare Hogarth House as soon as possible.

Quentin Bell states that Virginia was taken to a nursing home, presumably Burley, on 25th March, one day before publication of *The Voyage Out*, which had been delayed due to Virginia's illness. She stayed at the home for a week while Leonard prepared the house, and when she was brought to the house, she had four nurses to look after her. Leonard describes the terrifying first few weeks at Hogarth, going into detail about Virginia's incessant talking and having to be physically restrained. However, slowly, Virginia began to improve, and by the end of November 1915, the last nurse had left. Virginia often talked about her weight, which went up and down as a result of her illness:

> 'My difficulty is to find any clothes – my weight is 12 stones – Leonard says you weigh 13.10 – but this I don't believe. Anyhow I'm very well and enjoy sitting in this mound of flesh. I spend my spare time in bed, but I'm allowed out in the afternoons.'

Letter to Katherine Cox, 14 November 1915

> 'We are settled here again, and thank God, the last nurse is gone. So much of my energy went into making conversation that I feel better instantly. I am to be allowed to write, and gradually return to the world.'

Letter to Duncan Grant, 15 November 1915

Virginia's essay, *On Being Ill*, was published in 1926 in *The Criterion* magazine, founded by T.S. Eliot. In it, she compares illness with love, battle and jealousy as being the foremost themes of literature; or what they should be, as illness is hardly noticed in literature. She claims that illness seems to increase imagination and feeling, and that there is a childish outspokenness in illness, where truths are revealed.

Throughout her diaries, Virginia often talks about physical ill health, notably of when she needs to rest during her menstruation. There are headaches which can last for months, demonstrated by the gaps in the diaries, and touched upon when she was feeling well enough to write. There are frequent visits to the dentist, as well as Dr Ferguson, among others, looking at her high temperature, the possibility of pneumonia and influenza and her weakened heart. Even though she had numerous bouts of ill health, Leonard believed that Richmond was good for Virginia's health, and on occasions, her health stabilised and she was relatively happy:

'I'm afraid we shan't be able to come tonight, as I'm rather headachy and have to stay quiet, and Leonard is going to the House to hear the debate.'

Letter to Katherine Cox, 11 January 1916

At the beginning of 1916, Virginia was still recovering from the traumatic events of 1915, and it was evident that she was following orders from her doctor about not doing too much:

'I'm quite well again, and hope to come up very soon, if you're visible. But this week is rather full. We saw the Dr, who says that in time I shall be able to do much more, but it will be a long time; still, I feel amazingly well.'

Letter to Margaret Llewelyn Davies, 23 January 1916

Quite often, Leonard had to be away from Virginia for work, and she would write him letters assuring him that she was doing what she was supposed to do so that he didn't worry:

'This is just to tell you what a wonderfully good beast I am. I've done everything in order, not forgetting medicine twice. Fergusson came this morning, and said it was the best thing for me to get away tomorrow. He had been seeing Craig, who had sent a message to tell me to stay in bed every morning, and always have a sleeping draught at hand, to take at the least wakefulness – and altogether to be very careful for a fortnight. Fergy said my pulse was quite different from last summer – not only much steadier, but much stronger. I am to go on spraying my throat. He seemed very pleased with me.'

Letter to Leonard Woolf, 17 April 1916

Virginia's care not to alarm Leonard is also evident in a letter to Vanessa:

'I'm afraid I shall have to be rather careful about coming over, as Leonard has been in rather a state again, and I've promised to be very quiet. I feel all right, but I've gone down rather in weight though I still weigh only just under 10 stones.'

Letter to Vanessa Bell, 26 July 1917

When Virginia got her period, she would usually spend the day in bed, but now she had the Hogarth Press to focus on, she felt sure that she could still work and rest at the same time:

'Owing to the usual circumstances, I had to spend the day recumbent. However, this is much mitigated by printing, which I do from my bed on the sloping table.'

Diaries, 25 October 1917

'Today Saturday the usual reasons have kept me recumbent; in the mitigated form which allows setting up and distributing.'

Diaries, 24 November 1917

Her menstruation might not have stopped her from working, but they would often stop her from visiting friends and relatives:

> 'I suppose you did not get the letter I wrote saying that circumstances might make it impossible for me to come today – so they have – damn them.'

Letter to Clive Bell, 26 May 1919

Virginia was not usually a person to complain about her illnesses, and so the following excerpt from a letter to Vanessa is surprising:

> 'Did anyone ever suffer as I did? You might have seen my soul shrivelling like a – I cannot remember the image exactly, but it is something one does by rubbing a piece of sealing wax and then everything else curls up – as if in agony.'

Letter to Vanessa Bell, 18 June 1919

As Virginia got older and had more understanding of her mental health, she began to recognise the symptoms of an impending episode. Leonard also described the recurring symptoms of her illness in his autobiography, which today may have been diagnosed as bi-polar disorder, but for Virginia to recognise them herself is a great testament to her insight:

> 'I must note the symptoms of the disease, so as to know it next time. The first day one's miserable: the second happy.'

Diaries, 10 April 1921

> 'I must hurriedly note more symptoms of the disease, so that I can turn back here and medicine myself next time. Well; I'd worn through the acute stage, and come

to the philosophic semi depressed, indifferent, and spent the afternoon taking parcels round the shops, going to Scotland Yard for my purse…'

Diaries, 12 April 1921

In this next entry, Virginia admits to her diary that she is a jealous person, whether jealous of her sister's life or other people's success:

'Now I note the latest symptom – complete absence of jealousy. What I mean is that I shall feel instantly warm and pleased (not only after an hour and a sharp pang) if there's a long and sound and appreciative review of L in the Lit Sup tomorrow.'

Diaries, 13 April 1921

Acknowledging the symptoms of her mental illness was the first step, but then to do something about it would be the next. Virginia seemed to adhere to the doctor's advice that she had received years before – light exercise and rest:

'These, this morning, the first words I have written – to call it writing – for 60 days; and those days spent in wearisome headache, jumping pulse, aching back, frets, fidgets, lying awake, sleeping draughts, sedatives, digitalis, going for a little walk, and plunging back into bed again.'

Diaries, 8 August 1921

On some occasions, Virginia could be almost bedridden for months at a time, as this case in the summer of 1921:

'Far from being brilliant, I spent most of the summer in bed or on the verge of it, completely comatose. But then life is so pleasant when one gets up again.'

Letter to Lady Ottoline Morrell, 8 November 1921

Sir Leslie
Stephen.
Painting
by George
Frederic Watts
1878
National
Portrait Gallery

Julia Prinsep
Stephen with a
young Virginia
Stephen, 1884

Virginia and Adrian Stephen playing cricket, 1886

Gerald Duckworth, Virginia Stephen, Thoby Stephen,
Vanessa Stephen and George Duckworth (back row);
Adrian Stephen, Julia Prinsep Stephen and Leslie
Stephen (front row), 1892

Julia,
Leslie and
Virginia
Stephen
at Talland
House,
1892

Vanessa
and Virginia
Stephen,
1893

Vanessa
Stephen taken
by Beresford,
circa 1908

Thoby
Stephen
taken by
Beresford,
circa 1908

Virginia Stephen and Leonard Woolf on their
engagement, 1912

Adrian
and Karin
Stephen,
1914

Virginia Woolf and Katherine (Ka) Cox,
1912. Photo: Houghton Library, Harvard,
MS 57 (203)

Leonard
and Virginia
Woolf.
Hyde Park
June 1925.
Photo:
Sydney J.
Loeb

Hogarth House & Suffield House in
Paradise Road, Richmond

L-R: Lady Ottoline Morrell, Maria Nys, Lytton Strachey,
Duncan Grant, Vanessa Bell, 1915

Lytton Strachey and Saxon Sydney-Turner, 1917

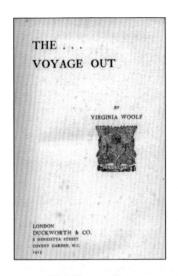

The Voyage Out
cover, 1915

Kew Gardens
cover, 1919

Virginia
Woolf,
Cornwall,
1916. Photo:
Houghton
Library,
Harvard, MS
Thr 559 (21)

Richmond Bridge in 1930s, Lloyd family album

Roger Fry and his wife Helen,
circa 1897

E.M.
Forster,
1917

Katherine
Mansfield,
1917

Margaret
Llewelyn
Davies,
circa 1920s

Duncan Grant (left) and John Maynard
Keynes, circa 1917 at Asheham House

Virginia Woolf with family and friends in the
garden at Monk's House

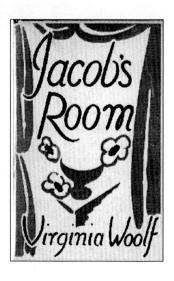

Monday or Tuesday,
published in 1921

Jacob's Room,
published in 1922

 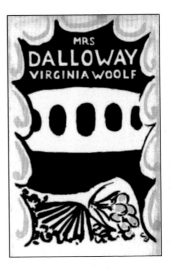

The Common Reader,
published 1925

Mrs Dalloway,
published 1925

Lytton Strachey, Virginia Woolf, Goldsworthy Lowes 1923.
Photo: Lady Ottoline Morrell
Houghton Library, Harvard, MS Thr 561 (0003)

Above: Dora Carrington, Ralph Partridge, Lytton
Strachey, Oliver Partridge, Frances Partridge, 1923
Below: T.S. Eliot with Virginia Woolf, 1924

Virginia with Pinka and Vita Sackville-West at Monk's House, 1933.
Photo: Houghton Library, Harvard, MS Thr 560 (103)

Life Magazine 1930

Time Magazine 1937

However, what makes the previous entry positive is that she is happy to be up and out of bed again. Nevertheless, when she wasn't suffering from mental exhaustion or laying recumbent with period issues, other illnesses would force Virginia back to bed:

> 'Tonight my reading begins' did I say? And two nights later I was shivering over the fire and had to tumble into bed with the influenza. How describe the fortnights lapse? Happily, it has been a mitigated lapse – not complete like the summer's.'

> Diaries, 22 January 1922

This particular bout of illness though, was to last longer than a fortnight:

> 'I'm now condemned to lie in bed for 2 or 3 weeks, until my heart gets right, which the influenza has put wrong. So letters are more than ever needed. I can't say that the disease is good for the brain.'

> Letter to Lady Robert Cecil, 11 February 1922

> 'No infection is left; only this damnable organ, always in my case as you know, so warm and loving, jumps by night, and gives me a slight temperature.'

> Letter to Violet Dickinson, 12 February 1922

A month later, Virginia was still not well, and her doctor came to see her. This slightly amusing entry finishes with a precursor to her elegy when leaving Hogarth House; 'when I was creeping about.':

> 'So far I had written that Monday when Fergusson came in and pronounced that my eccentric pulse had passed the limits of reason and was in fact insane. So I was laid in bed again, and set up my state in the

drawing room, where I now write sitting up in bed, alongside the fire, with a temperature a shade below normal, and a heart become naturally abnormal, so that perhaps I shall be up and creeping this time next week.'

Diaries, 14 February 1922

'But after 6 weeks influenza my mind throws up no matutinal fountains. My note book lies by my bed unopened. At first I could hardly read for the swarm of ideas that rose involuntarily.'

Diaries, 18 February 1922

With no improvement in her health, the couple decided to go and see a different doctor, and it seems that Virginia was getting frustrated:

'We are now driving into London to see another doctor, as my heart and my temperature still annoy me; and the dr here, wants to get it settled. I can't go on lying in bed.'

Letter to Violet Dickinson, 27 February 1922

Even though Virginia was still sick, visitors would still come and see her, but probably on the advice of the doctor not to tax herself with writing, Virginia goes into no detail about their visits in her diaries:

'Still invalided, I sit and receive visitors almost daily; and say nothing about them here.'

Diaries, 24 March 1922

The idea of normal has always been a difficult one for Virginia. Is having children normal? Is having a temperature of 99 normal?

I have discovered the secret of perfect health – to have a temperature of 99. I do this and feel better than I have ever felt in my life. The doctors must have been mistaken when they made the temperature normal.

Letter to Lady Ottoline Morrell, 3 April 1922

I no longer much enjoy the height of my temperature, and very much hope to be normal again.

Letter to Lady Ottoline Morrell, 16 May 1922

Virginia's frustration is evident in a letter to Violet Dickinson. Quite often, medical experts believed that pulling teeth would help alleviate symptoms of madness:

God knows what is happening to my influenza germs. I can't get rid of this miserable little temperature, and last week it flared up into another attack, and laid my heart flat again. So now they're going to pull 2 teeth.

Letter to Violet Dickinson, 18 May 1922

Although feeling better, doctors became concerned about the state of Virginia's heart, to which she quips:

I feel much better again – in fact, it wouldn't matter at all except for the heart, which seems to object. Why isn't one made rather more simply? Without a heart.

Letter to Janet Case, 21 May 1922

After more tests and doctor visits, diagnosis points to a problem with the lungs, and possibly pneumonia:

My temp. goes on, as usual, & Dr Hamill thinks that my right lung is suspicious. Fergusson says no. And perhaps I shall have to see Sainsbury to settle it.

Diaries, 17 July 1922

Hamill sticks to it that my right lung is wrong. Fergusson finds nothing. Pneumonia germs have been discovered. And my case is to be laid before Sainsbury on the 9th – all rather a bore.

Diaries, 22 July 1922

As Leonard comments in his autobiography, and through evidence of Virginia's own personal writing, she tended to get excited at thoughts of social interaction. The doctor would order her to remain calm:

"Equanimity - practise equanimity Mrs Woolf " he said, as I left; an unnecessary interview from my point of view; but we are forced into it by one step after another on the part of the bacteriologists. I take my temperature no more till Oct. 1st.

Diaries, 16 August 1922

The beginning of 1923 saw Virginia's friend and rival, Katherine Mansfield, die of tuberculosis, and her death would affect Virginia for the next few months. Virginia still had a high temperature, but tuberculosis was ruled out:

I go on having a mild temp. They vaccinated a guinea pig with my spittle. It died, but no one knows what of – anyhow not tuberculosis, which one idiot of a doctor discovered.

Letter to Violet Dickinson, 23 January 1923

One meeting with Ottoline Morrell would lead Virginia to the admission that she dislikes being taken care of:

She told me I looked wonderfully well, wh[ich] I disliked. Why? I wonder. Because I had had a headache perhaps, partly. But to be well and use strength to get more out of life is, surely, the greatest fun in the world.

What I dislike is feeling that I'm always taking care, or being taken of. Never mind – work, work.

Diaries, 4 June 1923

This period was one in which Leonard took on the role of carer for Virginia, helping her to manage her mental health and overseeing her medication, taking her to see numerous doctors and ensuring she took adequate rest when he noticed symptoms such as increased anxiety levels. The loneliness which Virginia must have felt as a person dealing with mental health problems must have been eased by knowing that she had Leonard by her side to help her.

Although ill health would plague Virginia for the rest of her life, it seems that she regained some of her strength from a more measured pace of life, going for regular long walks and breathing clean smog-free air while living in Richmond. The menstruation she often complained of demonstrated her body was well, and the physical work of typesetting, which she could do even when lying down, allowed her to channel nervous energy into something productive and satisfying. Above all, Richmond was where the couple developed as people, and as a team, helping each other with writing and editing, printing and publishing, making a comfortable home and entertaining their friends. Life in Richmond gave Virginia freedom in her writing, freedom to grow as a person and the freedom to think for herself again.

Virginia at her Leisure

I stayed in Paris by way of facing life. Yes, I clap the spurs to my flanks and see myself taking fences gallantly.

Diaries, 11 May 1923

Virginia's life in Richmond was a busy one. She was either helping Leonard with the Hogarth Press, writing reviews, journalism, short stories and novels or assisting with the local Women's Guild. There was entertaining to plan as numerous visitors took the train to Richmond to visit the couple and sometimes Virginia would go to London to meet her friends. What else did Virginia do to relax, and where did she go?

Virginia had enjoyed going on holiday since her childhood. In *A Passionate Apprentice*, Virginia's early journals, we can see that Cornwall was especially important for her. Spending many summers in the town of St. Ives, and specifically at Talland House, Virginia was greatly influenced by the area. Indeed, the lighthouse that inspired *To the Lighthouse*, Godrevy Lighthouse, could be seen from Talland House:

> When we reached the gate at Talland House, we should thrust it open and find ourselves among the familiar sights again.

A Passionate Apprentice, 11 August 1905

It seems that Viginia enjoyed going there. Boats trips and

excursions to places such as Land's End and the Gurnard's Head feature in her journals. Many years later, when she was writing *Sketch of the Past*, Virginia recalls these summers spent at Talland House:

> When they took Talland House father and mother gave us – me at any rate – what has been perennial, invaluable.

Sketch of the Past[1]

Pages of memories from these times spent in Cornwall adorn *Sketch of the Past;* here was Virginia's first retreat. It was a place where she could escape from London, no matter how drawn to the city she was. However, these happy times were to stop, as after her mother died, her father could not bear to stay in Talland House again, and so it was sold. However, Virginia often returned to Cornwall during her married life, feeling energised by the experience:

> Why am I so incredibly and incurably romantic about Cornwall? One's past I suppose: I see children running in the garden. A spring day. Life so new. People so enchanting.

Diaries, 22 March 1921

Virginia ventured further afield as a young woman. In 1906, she travelled with Vanessa and others through France and Italy to visit Greece and Turkey. Spending almost two months away, Virginia seemed enthralled by Greece especially. In 1908, she spent some time in Italy, and returned there, to Florence specifically, in 1909, soon after Lytton Strachey's marriage proposal.

After her marriage to Leonard Woolf in 1912, the couple visited Spain and Italy and thus her new life as Virginia Woolf began. In 1923, just one year before leaving Richmond,

Leonard and Virginia took another trip to Spain and France. During this time, she did not write in her diary, merely mentioning the trip on her return, but she wrote letters. They travelled to Madrid, Granada and Murcia in Spain, and then Paris, where Virginia stayed longer than Leonard as he was to take up new duties as editor of *The Nation and Atheneum*. Once again, as she tended to do, Virginia became enamoured with her surroundings at that time:

> Nevertheless I am determined never to live long in England again. The rapture of getting into warmth and colour and good sense and general congeniality of temper is so great.

Letter to Vanessa Bell from Granada, 1 April 1923

It is apparent that Virginia could be positively affected by her location, and that travelling to new places and seeing the sights enlivened her spirits.

Asheham House

While staying in Firle, Sussex, Leonard first saw Asheham House. Virginia had already moved to the Sussex countryside, having rented a cottage in the village of Firle, which she renamed Little Talland House; a flashback to happy times at Talland House in Cornwall. It was at this point in time that Virginia and Leonard were courting, and the idea of leasing Asheham House together was too good to resist. Virginia gave up Little Talland House after less than a year, and acquired a five-year lease on Asheham. Just like other places had affected Virginia, Asheham was no different:

> It was Ash[e]ham and its ghostly footsteps and whisperings which gave Virginia the idea for A Haunted House, and I can immediately see, hear and

smell the house when I read the opening words.

Beginning Again[2]

For Leonard, the house had a great personality, but it would be much more for Virginia. After her episode in Burley House, Twickenham in August 1913, it would be Asheham where Virginia would go to recover. In a letter to Leonard, she writes from Asheham:

> Dearest Mongoose, I wish you would believe how much I am grateful and repentant. You have made me so happy.

Letter to Leonard Woolf, 4 December 1913

Virginia would stay at Asheham for the majority of 1914, interrupted by a trip to Cornwall. Upon their return, the couple searched for a new place to live, and this is when they rented rooms at 17, The Green in Richmond. The house at Asheham remained their country retreat, but once again, in September 1915, the house became a recovery ward. Virginia's writing was restricted at this time, and she was only allowed to write short letters and notes. It seemed that Virginia stayed in Sussex until November, when she returned to Hogarth House.

In 1919, the couple were not allowed to renew the lease at Asheham, and therefore had to leave. They left Asheham at the end of August of that year, but in comparison to Virginia's feelings when she was leaving Richmond in 1924, there is no outpouring of affection for the house she was leaving:

> What struck me most was the farewell – every one feeling a little sentimental about Asheham.

Letter to Vanessa Bell, 29 August 1919

Monk's House

By this time, however, the couple had already bought and sold the Round House, and bought Monk's House at auction. The Round House was bought spur of the moment in June 1919, but the couple saw Monk's House being advertised for sale at auction and decided to bid for it. Their bid was successful and it was bought in July. They sold the Round House in the same month. Monk's House was to be their home for the rest of their lives. Leonard himself acknowledges in *Downhill All the Way* that the place in which the couple lived was the most influential aspect of their lives:

> In each case the most powerful moulder of them [the couple] and of their lives was the house in which they lived.

Downhill All the Way[3]

For Leonard, both Monk's House and Hogarth House were equally important for Virginia and her well-being. He describes both as having a continuity of people living in them. For Virginia, although possibly sarcastically, her first comments about Monk's House were not as positive as those she had about Hogarth House:

> Monk's House will be perhaps the ugliest house in Sussex – not plain ugliness either, but cultured ugliness, which is worse.

Letter to Vanessa Bell, 17 July 1919

However, just a few days later in a letter to Janet Case, Virginia writes:

> This is going to be the pride of our hearts; I warn you;

186

and I see already we talk a great deal too much for our friends.

Letter to Janet Case, 23 July 1919

What Virginia is referring to here, is the garden at Monk's House. This was the main reason for buying the house. The garden was so loved that Virginia set up a writing room towards the rear of the garden, so she could look out while she was working. The inside of the house Virginia was either not so fond of, or embarrassed about. In letters to T.S. Eliot and Vita Sackville-West, four years apart, Virginia warned about the discomforts of Monk's House:

> We would like to ask you and Mrs Eliot down here for a week end. The only thing is that the discomfort is so great and arrangements so primitive that I don't think she would find it possible.

Letter to T.S. Eliot, 28 July 1920

> I ought to warn you of the inconveniences and discomforts of this house, especially when it rains, but they are too many to begin on.

Letter to Vita Sackville-West, 31 August 1924

This, of course, does not mean to say that Virginia disliked living in Rodmell; it seemed to be her way to discredit a place and then profess love for it a moment later – just like she did with Richmond. Monk's House was to be a sanctuary for Virginia until she died. She left the house on March 28th 1941 and walked to the nearby River Ouse, where she weighed her pockets down with stones and drowned herself. Some local children found her body three weeks later.

Monk's House can still be visited today as it is now a museum run by the National Trust, where the highlights include Virginia's bedroom and her writing lodge set in the gardens that she loved. The website for the house is www. nationaltrust.org.uk/Monk's-house.

Charleston House

Charleston, was the Sussex home of Vanessa Bell and Duncan Grant which they took in 1916. Charleston was certainly a meeting house, and one where a lot of the Bloomsbury Group would gather together. Indeed, it has been called the country focus of the Bloomsbury Group. It was most likely Virginia who convinced Vanessa to take the house. She was living at both Asheham House and Hogarth House at the time, and in May 1916, wrote passionately to Vanessa:

> I wish you'd leave Wisset and take Charleston....
> it's a most delightful house... but it sounds a most
> attractive place – and 4 miles from us, so you wouldn't
> be badgered by us.

Letter to Vanessa Bell, 14 May 1916

Charleston was indeed taken by Vanessa, and Virginia and the rest of her family and friends would enjoy it for many years. At Charleston, the artists who lived there painted the walls and decorated the furniture, with many of the designs which were inspired by the French painters introduced by Roger Fry.

Today, Charleston remains as a testament to their ideas and talent, housing many of their original designs and paintings. It serves as a wonderful literary and arts centre offering a variety of events throughout the year, celebrating not only the rich heritage of work by members of the Bloomsbury Group but also offering a platform for established and emerging artists and writers today.

www.charleston.org.uk

Woolf on War

We were kept awake last night by New Year Bells. At first
I thought they were ringing for victory.

Diaries, 1 January 1915

As has been mentioned earlier in this book, Virginia and Leonard moved to Richmond in 1914, just after the war had started. The war affected millions of people all over the world, as reinforcements were drawn from young men living in far-flung British colonies to take part in the ongoing conflict.

Virginia was deeply affected by the war, mainly because both she and Leonard were pacifists and believed that dialogue was the only way to resolve international conflict and they watched in horror to see so many young men being slaughtered or coming back wounded or traumatised by their experiences. In 1916, in a letter to Margaret Llewelyn Davies, she writes 'I become steadily more feminist, owing to the *Times*, which I read at breakfast and wonder how this preposterous masculine fiction keeps going a day longer – without some vigorous young woman pulling us together and marching through it'[1], thus professing her pacifism and distaste for the war. The masculine fiction to which she refers is the war. A lot of Virginia's writing was influenced by the war, whether fact or fiction. She wrote a review of *The War from the Street* by D. Bridgman Metchim, in which she states that '...the history of the war is not and never will be written from our point of view.'[2]

Her novels too, show how much the war influenced her. In *Jacob's Room*, the protagonist, Jacob Flanders (whose surname evokes Flanders Field in Belgium, where many lives were lost), is killed in action on the front. As a post-war novel, it focuses on the new modernist world. The novel follows the life of Jacob, as he grows up, goes to Cambridge and then on to his travels in Italy and Greece. The fate of Jacob is sealed when he is called up for duty and is killed on the battlefield. *Jacob's Room* was Virginia's first foray into the experimental novel. It does not follow the concept of bildungsroman; Jacob does not necessarily come of age, but he dies. His death is really only mentioned indirectly:

> 'He left everything just as it was,' Bonamy marvelled. 'Nothing arranged. All his letters strewn about for anyone to read. What did he expect? Did he think he would come back?' he mused, standing in the middle of Jacob's room.

Jacob's Room[3]

The narrative of *Jacob's Room* is very fragmentary, building Jacob's life from the point of view of the women around him; indeed, the novel begins and ends with the words of his mother, Betty Flanders.

Mrs Dalloway, another post-war novel, includes the character Septimus Smith, an ex-soldier, probably suffering from what we would now classify as Post Traumatic Stress Disorder (PTSD), and he eventually throws himself out of a window, landing onto iron spikes; this could be seen as a reference to Virginia's own suicide attempt when, overcome with grief, she jumped out of a window but survived.

In *To the Lighthouse*, Andrew Ramsay is also killed in action. Andrew is the eldest of the sons in the novel, and he is young and independent. His death is announced bluntly, which could be seen to echo the immediacy of the war and its unfortunate results:

> A shell exploded. Twenty or thirty young men were blown up in France, among them Andrew Ramsay, whose death, mercifully, was instantaneous.

To The Lighthouse[4]

The war also affected Virginia personally, as well as professionally. Her husband, Leonard, was called up to war. Firstly, as he was his wife's primary carer, it was decided that Virginia was too ill for him to go; in addition, he suffered from a trembling hand, so he was exempted from duty. The second time he was called up, the same reasons applied. However, Leonard's brothers, Cecil and Philip Woolf were not so fortunate, and they were both called up with his brother Cecil being killed. Like thousands of other families, the terrible loss of life on the battlefields, could never be far from their thoughts.

From her diary and letters, Virginia talks about hiding, or sleeping in the cellar to escape the air raids, as well as the lack of rations. Once peace had been announced, she felt it her duty to go out and celebrate, but as can be seen, she did not really enjoy the celebrations; seeing it more as a noisy debacle.

The first quote mentioned here is from Virginia's diary, describing hearing about a British warship, and mistaking the sirens for the beginning of peace. In fact, she was listening to the fate of HMS Formidable, launched in 1898 but sunk by two German torpedoes on January 1st 1915. Virginia would often record such events, including the various raids and the sirens acknowledging the threat, as well as zeppelin raids:

Half way home we heard "British warship...British warship" and found that the Formidable had been sunk in the channel. We were kept awake last night by New Year Bells. At first I thought they were ringing for victory.

Diaries, 1 January 1915

On the same date as the fate of HMS Formidable, there was a fatal train crash at Ilford, Essex, which Virginia reported on. What was important about the story that *The Times* ran on the event was that the war was teaching the British people the value of human life:

The Times has a queer article upon a railway smash, in which it says that the war has taught us a proper sense of proportion with respect to human life. I have always thought we priced it absurdly high; but I never thought the Times would say so.

Diaries, 5 January 1915

As in the previous chapter, many people visited Virginia and often spent hours talking. Maynard Keynes had dinner with the Woolfs, and the talk turned to the subject of war:

Then we [And Maynard Keynes] talked about the war. We aren't fighting now, he says, but only waiting for the spring...We are bound to win - and in great style too, having at the last moment applied all our brains and all our wealth to the problem.

Diaries, 20 January 1915

It is very possible that the final comments are sarcastic; it appears that the British government 'lavished' money on the war. Whether Maynard and Virginia thought this was a good thing is difficult to say, but the tone of the entry suggests they were opposed to it.

When Leonard feared that he would be called to duty, he went to see his doctor and friend, Maurice Wright, about his trembling hands. The doctor knew all about Virginia's situation, and eventually gave Leonard a medical certificate stating that he had 'definite nervous disabilities'[5] which would prevent him from active service. Leonard was indeed called up, and on May 30th 1916, he went for his medical. After being stripped and examined, he produced the certificate from Dr Wright and was exempted from all forms of military service. Upon being called up again in 1917, Leonard was once more exempted from duty. Unfortunately for his two brothers, Cecil and Philip, the war would be a tragedy. Both were sent for military service and while Cecil was killed by a shell in the Battle of Cambrai in 1917, his brother Philip was wounded by the same shell.

At a time when a lot of young men were being called up for duty, it was inevitable that Virginia's friends would be affected by this. Friends such as Lytton Strachey, David Garnett and Duncan Grant were all put before tribunals to argue their cases as conscientious objectors, and Virginia wrote to Lady Robert Cecil to help argue their cases:

> Duncan Grant the painter, who is a conscientious objector and will be coming before the Central Tribunal in a week or two. If you don't mind and felt that you could possibly say anything on his behalf to Lord Salisbury who is on the Tribunal, I would send you details in a day or two.

Letter to Lady Robert Cecil, 3 June 1916

In a later letter, Virginia thanks Lady Cecil (Nelly) for any influence she might have had and also to announce the harsh reality of the war:

The war is a nightmare isn't it – two cousins of mine were killed this last week, and I suppose in other families it's much worse.

Letter to Lady Robert Cecil, 16 June 1916

By now, the threat of being bombed was incredibly real, and Virginia carefully recorded in her diary and her letters details of some of these events:

16 German aeroplanes have just passed over Richmond – They haven't done us any harm – We went and sat in the cellar and listened to them, and Nelly nearly had hysterics. The people next door saw them perfectly from the top window. A man in the street says one has been brought down in the Park – They sounded quite near, but I don't know if they dropped bombs or whether it was only our guns. Carrington has just rung up to say there were 35 over Gordon S[quare] but didn't drop bombs.

Letter to Vanessa Bell, 6 October 1917

Later in October 1917, Britain was to be hit by the last Zeppelin raid of the First World War, which occurred over two nights; October 19th and 20th. In this raid, the department store Swan and Edgar was destroyed:

We heard two soft distant but unmistakable shocks about 9.30; then a third which shook the window; then silence. It turns out a Zeppelin came over, hovered unseen for an hour or two and left. We heard no more of it.

Diaries, 20 October 1917

We had Zeppelins over last night. They are said to have destroyed Swan and Edgar at Piccadilly.

> We only heard the guns at a distance, and never heard the warning at all.

Letter to Vanessa Bell, 20 October 1917

On December 6th 1917, a large amount of bombs were to fall on the capital and surrounding areas. Virginia describes being woken up by her husband and going downstairs to sit with Nellie and Lottie. Virginia could hear the guns, apparently heading towards Barnes. After the sounds got more distant, the four residents decided to go back to bed. However:

> In ten minutes there was no question of staying there: guns apparently at Kew. Up we jumped, more hastily this time, since I remember leaving my watch, and trailing cloak and stockings behind me. Servants apparently calm and even jocose. In fact one talks through the noise.

Diaries, 6 December 1917

It is clear from the previous entry that by the end of 1917, Virginia was becoming used to the regime of hiding from the air raids; event the servants were apparently in a jovial mood. This continues in a letter about two weeks' later:

> We had a raid last night – Bob was dining with us and talked so loud that we couldn't hear the guns; but Saxon says it was rather bad in London. We ate most of our dinner in the coal cellar.

Letter to Vanessa Bell, 19 December 1917

This idea of continuing a dinner party during an air raid is echoed in a diary entry in early 1918:

> Nelly burst in to say that the Take Cover had sounded.

So we had our dinner partly in the cellar; Bob talking at such a rate that it was necessary to listen at the window for the guns, loud enough though they were.

Diaries, 3 January 1918

Throughout the war, rumours of peace would surface every now and again, but it seemed to Virginia that these rumours came in swathes and then fell distant again:

This talk of peace…comes to the surface with a kind of tremor of hope once in 3 months; then subsides; then swells again. What it now amounts to, one doesn't even like to guess, having a sort of superstition about guessing: at any rate, one can't help feeling something moving.

Diaries, 4 January 1918

The hope of peace all broken up again; policies once more a running in every direction, so far as one can tell.

Diaries, 12 January 1918

After a short break in air raids, they came again towards the end of January. Having now experienced numerous raids, Virginia questions whether it is boredom or fear that leads the couple to wander about their house:

From 8 to 1.15 we roamed about, between coal hole kitchen bedroom and drawing room. I don't know how much is fear, how much boredom; but the result is uncomfortable, most of all, I believe, because one must talk bold and jocular small talk for 4 hours with the servants to ward off hysteria.

Diaries, 28 January 1918

Unfortunately, the night of January 28th 1918 wasn't going to be the last raid, and London was hit again the following day. This time, the danger came very close to Virginia:

> This time it began at 9.10: the warning at least. It was far louder this time. An aeroplane went over the house about 11.30. Soon after, the guns were so near that I didn't like to fetch a pair of shoes left in the bedroom. We had arranged mattresses in the kitchen and after the first noise slackened we lay all together, L on the kitchen table, like a picture of slum life. One thud came very near; but in an hour we had the bugles, and went up to bed. The thud, which L distinguished from the rest, came from the explosion of bombs at Kew. Nine people, I think killed. Servants became plaintive, and Lottie began talking of the effect upon her head; they hint that we ought to leave London.

> Diaries, 29 January 1918

> Well, you almost lost me. Nine bombs on Kew; 7 people killed in one house, a hotel crushed.

> Letter to Vanessa Bell, 29 January 1918

What seems clear about the previous entry is that Virginia and her servants continue bonding through necessity. However, they talked together and with Lottie's suggestion, it seems that the servants were comfortable enough in the presence of Virginia and Leonard to give advice.

On the evening on March 8th 1918, Virginia was in bed when she suddenly heard an explosion. She thought that it couldn't be another raid, but instead the sound came from a bus. Unfortunately, the whistles sounded and they heard guns:

> So we got our things together & went to the kitchen. This was at 11.30. Looking out we could only see stars

yellowish in some sort of mist; no moon; but a still night. As we lay down on our mattresses there was a great though distant explosion.

Diaries, 8 March 1918

As well as the rumours of peace, there were many other stories being told as well, but whether these were true or not is unclear. The following extract is quite shocking, and even Virginia thought that it was horrific:

L was told the other day that the raids are carried out by women. Women's bodies were found in the wrecked aeroplanes. They are smaller and lighter, and thus leave more room for bombs. Perhaps it's sentimental, but the thought seems to me to add a particular touch of horror.

Diaries, 7 June 1918

As the war was coming to a close, the hope for peace for Virginia was profound, and in her usual way, described in beautiful language:

But their Retreat goes on, & last night, beautiful, cloudless, still & moonlit, was to my thinking the first of peace, since one went to bed fairly positive that never again in all our lives need we dread the moonlight.

Diaries, 18 October 1918

After many years of hiding in cellars and kitchens, peace was officially announced on November 11th 1918. Virginia was staying in Richmond at the time of the announcement:

Twenty five minutes ago the guns went off, announcing peace. A siren hooted on the river. They are hooting still. A few people ran to look out of windows.

The rooks wheeled round, and were for a moment, the symbolic look of creatures performing some ceremony, partly of thanksgiving, partly of valediction over the grave.

Diaries, 11 November 1918

Although Virginia was happy that the country was now at peace, she did not seem to enjoy all the celebrations that were going on around her, but she is pleased that Vanessa's new baby will be born into a peaceful country:

The guns have been going off for half an hour, and the sirens whistling; so I suppose we are at peace, and I can't help being glad that your precious imp will be born into a moderately reasonable world. I see we're not going to be allowed any quiet all day.

Letter to Vanessa Bell, 11 November 1918

Through all of the war and the advent of peace, it was easy to see that Virginia was still thinking about writing and matters of literature:

The question of peace is an extremely interesting one. We literary people have been comparing our feelings a good deal. Desmond heard the news early in the morning, and went straight to Buckingham Palace. He says the crowd was very good there, and they had bands, and climbed all over the Victoria memorial, pulling themselves up by her nose and breasts; then the King and Queen came out; like two little dolls.

Letter to Vanessa Bell, 19 November 1918

I am overwhelmed with things that I ought to have written about; peace dropped like a great stone into my pool, & the eddies are still rippling out to the further bank.

Diaries, 21 November 1918

Virginia was rather underwhelmed with Armistice Day, mainly due to the noise of the celebrations, which seems ironic as she had become used to the sounds of the air raids. In July 1919, Britain held Peace Day, which was to be a bank holiday to celebrate the end of the war. In a similar way to November 11th the previous year, Virginia was not entirely impressed, especially with the procession in Richmond in which she thought nobody would want to see dignitaries all dressed up. However, the final quotation here demonstrates that after thinking about the situation, she decided that she should get involved. From what she describes, it appears that it was to be a good decision:

> One ought to say something about Peace day, I suppose, though whether its worth taking a new nib for that purpose I don't know. I'm sitting wedged into the window, & so catch almost on my head the steady drip of rain which is pattering on the leaves. In ten minutes or so the Richmond procession begins.

Diaries, 19 July 1919

> After sitting though the procession and the peace bells unmoved, I began after dinner, to feel that if something was going on, perhaps one had better be in it... Red and green and yellow and blue balls rose slowly into the air... Rising over the Thames, among trees, these rockets were beautiful.

Diaries, 20 July 1919

The devastating effect of the First World War on an entire generation cannot be underestimated. Women had carried out many of the jobs previously undertaken by men during the war and the government could no longer ignore the suffragists' demands for equal rights. In 1918, some women had been granted the right to vote, many had been left widowed or orphaned. The number of men available for the workforce was drastically reduced and the economy desperately needed women's labour to recover.

The suffering and deprivation of the war years would give way to an exciting new decade —The Roaring Twenties — in which young women took advantage of the new freedoms on offer. Virginia Woolf would benefit too from the new confidence among women, and the possibility to have a voice in society.

Leonard's Viewpoint

Virginia and I celebrated the end of a civilization and the beginning of peace by sitting in the lovely, panelled room in Hogarth House, Richmond.

Downhill All the Way[1]

Leonard Woolf was born on November 25th 1880 to Marie de Jongh and Sidney Woolf. He was the third-born child of ten. The young Leonard attended St Paul's School in London before going to Trinity College at Cambridge in 1899. He became friends with people such as Lytton Strachey and Thoby Stephen, and it is through Thoby, that he met Virginia. Leonard graduated in 1904, and acquired employment within the Colonial Civil Service, and was posted to Ceylon (Sri Lanka). He stayed there for seven years, and on his return to England in 1911, he used his personal experiences to write *The Village in the Jungle* (1913).

In *Beginning Again*, detailing the years from 1911 to 1918, he describes meeting Virginia again in July 1911, where he says that some things hadn't changed, including the extraordinary beauty of the two Miss Stephens. Although he states that Vanessa was usually more beautiful, he also writes that when Virginia was 'well, unworried, happy, amused, and excited, her face lit up with an intense almost ethereal beauty.'[2]. He goes on; 'Virginia is the only person whom I have known intimately who had the quality which one had to call genius.'

Already, at this early stage in their relationship, Leonard was demonstrating signs of the love which was to last throughout Virginia's life and beyond. It seems from Leonard's writing that he was unsure about what to do with his feelings for Virginia. He was intending on returning abroad but kept questioning whether he should ask her to marry him; 'By the end of 1911 I knew that I was in love with Virginia and that I should have to make up my mind rapidly what I was to do about it.' In early 1912, after some time away in Somerset, Leonard had made his mind up, and returned to London to ask Virginia to marry him, to which she replied that she needed some time before she could decide. Leonard resigned from his job on May 20th 1912, and on the 29th, Virginia told him that she loved him and would marry him. They were married on August 10th at St Pancras registry office.

Leonard was a successful writer in his own right, publishing many titles through his career, including *The Framework of a Lasting Peace* (1917) and *International Co-operative Trade* in 1922. He was also a contributor to *The New Statesman*, editor of *The Nation and Atheneum* and editor of *The Political Quarterly*.

Both his and Virginia's writings attest to the fact that he was essential to her mental health, and constantly looked after her while she was ill. In fact, it was his decision for the couple not to have children as this might have affected Virginia's mental health adversely. He was also the first reader of her writing – giving her invaluable feedback on her work. In, possibly, her last ever letter written, Virginia writes to Leonard: 'I want to tell you that you have given me complete happiness. No one could have done more than you have done. Please believe that.'

In researching this book, it has been surprising to read how Virginia and Leonard talked about the same events in very different ways. For example, describing the first time the couple saw Hogarth House, or when they first moved to Richmond – even their reasons for moving to Richmond. However, Leonard was writing his autobiographies many years after the facts, whereas Virginia was writing down her thoughts at the very moment of them happening. What we can see in Leonard's personal writing is a more considered approach to events. In Virginia's writing, she was often writing about different events at the same time and used very emotive language. As the reader can see, Leonard's main motive for moving to Richmond was to give Virginia the peace that she needed, whether she knew it or not. Richmond was to be her sanctuary:

> For we continued to live in Richmond mainly to protect her from London and the devastating disorientation which would threaten her social life if we returned to live there. It was a perpetual struggle to find the precarious balance of health for her among the strains and stresses of writing and society. The routine of everyday life had to be regular and rather rigid.

> *Downhill All the Way*[3]

Leonard considers having a strict routine to be important, and this was something that Virginia had possibly not had in her life since she was a child. Even in childhood, her routine was destroyed by family deaths and abuse. After their marriage, they decided to find a new place to live, and Richmond was chosen as it was close enough to central London to enable Virginia to be satisfied, but also far enough away from it so it was not a distraction. Richmond, clearly, had an effect on Leonard too:

> Eventually we took rooms at 17 The Green, Richmond, temporarily, meaning to find a house in Richmond. We

moved in on October 16. In 1914, before the motor car had destroyed its beauty and peace, Richmond Green was a charming place to live in.

Beginning Again[4]

The house on The Green was the one owned and run by Mrs le Grys, the Belgian landlady, and this was to be the start of Virginia's recovery that Leonard had hoped for:

> We settled down in Richmond and it seemed as if things were going well. We decided to try to find a house in Richmond and towards the end of 1914 we went to see Hogarth House in Paradise Road and fell in love with it. It was very beautiful.

Beginning Again[5]

Hogarth House was indeed to be Virginia's saviour. This charming house would give her so much, but there were still some troubled waters ahead. Leonard's description of the house fades into comparison with Virginia's – 'the nicest house in England'. What we don't get from Virginia is an intimate description of the house, but Leonard provided this in *Downhill all the Way*:

> The interior of the original undivided house must have been perfect. All the rooms were panelled, the ones on the ground floor with a certain amount of chaste ornamentation; in the others the panels became progressively plainer as one went up from floor to floor. Every room was beautifully proportioned.

> Occasionally one comes across a house upon which those who built it or lived in it have imposed a character and form markedly and specifically its own, as though it were a person or a work of art. Hogarth House was one of these. All the rooms, even when

we first saw them in the dirty, dusty desolation of an empty house, had beauty, repose, peace and yet life.

In the room itself one felt the security from anything like a hostile world, the peace and quiet, in this tremendous solidity of walls, doors and windows, and yet nothing could have been more light and graceful, more delicately and beautifully proportioned than the room itself.

Downhill All the Way[6]

This beautiful description of Hogarth House makes it clear to the reader that the couple adored the house. It is interesting to note that Leonard writes about feeling secure within the rooms, as this house was to be Virginia's safe place; the house that she could trust. In a similar way to Virginia humanising the house when it was time to leave, Leonard also describes the house 'as though it were a person'; a surrogate baby with a character of its own. Leonard managed to get the lease for Hogarth House and the move was set. However, one of the darkest periods in Virginia's health was about to begin:

I obtained a lease and we were to move in in March. Virginia's health seemed to have improved and she had begun to work and write again… Then quite suddenly in the middle of February there was again catastrophe… It was the beginning of the terrifying second stage of her mental breakdown.

It was necessary to get Hogarth House ready for us to move into immediately, to take our furniture which was being warehoused and put it into the house and find servants… The first fortnight was indeed terrifying. For a time Virginia was very violent with the nurses. The violence then subsided a little, but she began to talk incessantly.

After another day the stream of words diminished and finally she fell into a coma. I had a Richmond doctor, one of the best G.P's I have ever known, and the mental specialist, Maurice Craig, came down several times from London. They assured me, even when she was completely unconscious in the coma, that she would recover. They were right. When she came out of the coma, she was exhausted, but much calmer; then very slowly she began to recover.

Beginning Again[7]

This period of ill health must have been terrifying for Leonard, especially as Virginia would fall into a coma:

In the atmosphere of both houses, Monk's House in Rodmell and Hogarth House in Richmond, there was something similar. In both one felt a quiet continuity of people living.

The year 1915 with its private nightmare dragged itself slowly to an end. Meanwhile the public nightmare of the war also dragged itself on, but became continually more oppressive and terrible. In the first year of the war I was so entangled in the labyrinth of Virginia's illness – the psychological struggle, the perpetual problems of nurses and doctors, the sense of shifting insecurity – that I do not think that I had time to consider my own personal relation to the war and the fighting. But as the year waned and the fighting waxed and Virginia gradually grew better, I was forced to consider my position.

Beginning Again[8]

However, once settled into Hogarth House, Virginia was able to recover:

> In the last two years of the war Virginia's health became gradually more stable. She was writing again strenuously and regularly. She was at work on *Night and Day* and finished it at the end of 1918, and she also from time to time wrote short pieces like the *Mark on the Wall*.

Beginning Again[9]

The advent of the Hogarth Press was certainly something that aided Virginia's recovery:

> We were both interested in printing and had from time to time in a casual way talked about the possibility of learning to print. It struck me that it would be a good thing if Virginia had a manual occupation of this kind which, in say the afternoons, would take her mind completely off her work.

Beginning Again[10]

Leonard's plan of distracting Virginia from the stress of writing and sending her work to outside publishers was a good one. Having publishers read and criticise her work was very difficult for Virginia as the process tended to heighten her anxiety. Their printing endeavour would allow Virginia the freedom to publish her own work without fear of being criticised before it was published. The process of writing for Virginia was intense, as we learn from Leonard:

> I have never known anyone work with more intense, more indefatigable concentration than Virginia. This was particularly the case when she was writing a novel. The novel became part of her and she herself was absorbed into the novel. She wrote only in the

morning from 10 to 1 and usually she typed out in the afternoon what she had written by hand in the morning.

Beginning Again[11]

For this writing process to be effective, Virginia would need a quiet and focused working area, which she obviously found in Hogarth House as well as her writing room in the garden of Monk's House:

> She was an untidy writer…In Virginia's workroom there was always a very large, solid, plain wooden table… She very rarely sat at this table, and certainly never when she was writing a novel in the morning. To write her novel of a morning she sat in a very low armchair…; on her knees was a large board made of plywood which had an inkstand glued to it.

Downhill All the Way[12]

Leonard's description here is a valuable insight as to how Virginia worked. Towards the end of the war, Virginia was able to write more fluently, and Leonard recollects the moment he heard that peace had been announced:

> At 11 in the morning of Monday, November 11, 1918, I was writing in my room in Richmond when the maroons, as they were called, were fired. From this we knew that the armistice had been signed and that the Great War had ended. Virginia celebrated the return of peace by going to the dentist in Harley Street and I restlessly followed her.

Beginning Again[13]

Visiting the dentist seems to be an unusual way of celebrating the end of a war, but it was thought that bacteria in the mouth were connected to mental illness in some way, so regular visits would have been considered important to staying well. However, the years at Richmond were essential for Virginia, not only for her health, but also for her development as a writer. This is something that Leonard acknowledges:

> In 1919 we still had six years of life in Hogarth House before we moved into London. Those six years were, I am sure, crucial for the stabilizing of her mind and health and for her work, and I am quite sure that the tranquil atmosphere of these two houses… helped to tranquilize her mind.

Downhill All the Way[14]

These years of relative stability, development of the Hogarth Press and Virginia's recovery were of the utmost importance. As Virginia noted in her diary, nowhere else could they have started the Hogarth Press. Leonard attests to the fact that Richmond was extremely beneficial to the writer that Virginia would become:

> In the period with which I am now concerned, our years at Richmond from 1919 to 1924, her writing was strictly rationed and often interrupted. They were years of crucial importance in her development as a novelist, for during them she revolted against the methods and form of contemporary fiction.

Downhill All the Way[15]

As the Hogarth Press began to be more successful, the couple were very busy with printing. The distractions of central London were no longer integral to Virginia's sense of happiness. She often wrote that she was the happiest she had ever been, and this was the result of living and working in Richmond. However, as her health recovered, it became apparent that the couple's social life was getting more intense and the desire to move back to central London became more important for Virginia:

> In the four years 1920 to 1923, as Virginia's health grew more stable, our social life increased and became more and more of a problem. Our taste in human beings was pretty much the same, but we did not always agree about the best way of seeing them. Virginia loved 'Society', its functions and parties, the bigger the better; but she also liked – at any rate in prospect – any party.

Downhill All the Way[16]

It seems that the Richmond years were almost too successful in getting Virginia back to health. She might not have realised it, but Richmond was going to be the most important period in her life in terms of health and professional development, but the social life was calling her:

> Virginia always thought she was going to enjoy a party enormously before she went to it and quite often she did. I did not share her optimism, nor, therefore, ever quite so keenly her disappointments, and, though I sometimes enjoyed parties, I never felt the exhilaration which they sometimes gave to her. When we were still living in Richmond, she wrote in her diary that she and I were becoming celebrities and that I denied this, but then I had not, as she had, gone to Logan Pearsall Smith's tea-party in Chelsea or to the weekend with Ottoline Morrell at Garsington.

Downhill All the Way[17]

For Virginia, parties and a social life were very important and now she was recovering, the thrill of being at the centre of a social circle was once more integral to her happiness.

For Leonard, this was a dangerous position to be in:

> It was parties like this and our increasing sociability in London which made the question of whether we should stay on in Richmond or immigrate to Bloomsbury more and more urgent.

> ...I had been against a move, solely because I feared the result on Virginia's health. It had become much more stable, but it could never be neglected or ignored, and nothing was more dangerous for it than the mental fatigue produced by society and its social pleasures.

> In Richmond it was possible to keep some control over our social life and, at a danger signal, to shut ourselves off from it for a time. I feared that this would prove impossible in London.

> *Downhill All the Way*[18]

Leonard was keenly aware of the dangers of moving back to central London. However, the couple still had possession of Monk's House, which still offered a quiet place to retreat. As Leonard points out, Virginia was very much affected by her surroundings:

> Virginia was the least political animal that has lived since Aristotle invented the definition, though she was not a bit like the Virginia Woolf who appears in many books written by literary critics or autobiographers who did not know her, a frail invalidish lady living in an ivory tower in Bloomsbury and worshipped by a little clique of aesthetes. She was intensely interested in things, people, and events, and, as her new books show, highly sensitive to the atmosphere which surrounded her, whether it was personal, social or historical. She was therefore the last person who could

ignore the political menaces under which we all lived.

Downhill All the Way[19]

Leonard recognises how much they both changed and grew as people during their years in Richmond:

> The Leonard and Virginia who lived in Hogarth House, Richmond, from 1915 to 1924 were not the same people who lived in 52 Tavistock Square from 1924 to 1939.

Downhill All the Way[20]

> The development of the Hogarth Press was bound up with the development of Virginia as a writer and with her literary or creative psychology. When we moved from Hogarth House, Richmond to 52 Tavistock Square on March 13 1924, the Hogarth Press had published 32 books in the seven years of its existence.

Downhill All the Way[21]

Leonard has been accused by some writers of being overly controlling of Virginia, but her letters and his autobiography reveal a couple who liked working together, enjoyed socialising with friends, loved their garden at Monk's House and often went on holiday together. Leonard was certainly important in enabling Virginia to write, supporting her emotionally and managing their affairs financially too.

A Lasting Legacy

If statues and marble are solid to the touch, so, simply, are words resonant to the ear.[1]

An impression of the new statue

This book has been published in association with the successful campaign to erect the first, full figure, life-size bronze statue of Virginia Woolf in Richmond, to celebrate the ten years that Virginia and Leonard spent living in the town. Initiated by Cheryl Robson, the local council in Richmond has granted planning permission to install the statue on the terraces at Richmond Riverside in 2022. As Virginia referred to the River Thames at Richmond as 'her river', this is the perfect location for such a statue. The statue features Virginia sitting on a bench in a relaxed manner, gazing towards the river. This design creates an interactive artwork for people to enjoy.

The sculptor is award-winning Laury Dizengremel, who was commissioned to create a statue of Capability Brown, which has been installed on Hammersmith Riverside, gazing out over another stretch of the Thames. Her many works can be seen across the globe.

Virginia Woolf is regarded as one of the co-founders of Modernist Literature along with Irish writer, James Joyce, who was experimenting at the same time with the idea of 'stream of consciousness' in the novel, in works such as *Ulysses* (1922). James Joyce has been honoured with a full size statue, sculpted by Marjorie Fitzgibbon, in Earl Street, Dublin, since 1990.

Although there was an unveiling of a new statue of Millicent Fawcett in Parliament Square, as 2018 marks the centenary of the Representation of the People Act when some women were allowed to vote, there are very few statues of historical, non-royal women. In an article published by *The New Statesman* in March 2016, it was reported that a mere 2.7% of public statues are representations of historical, non-royal women.

> The statues of London are lovable; and the sparrows find the top hats of statesmen good lodging for their nests.[2]

The most famous representation of Virginia Woolf in London is the bust cast from a 1931 sculpture by Stephen Tomlin in Tavistock Square, near to where she moved after leaving Richmond. This was erected in June 2004 by the Virginia Woolf Society of Great Britain. Naturally, there are also representations of Woolf at Monk's House in Rodmell. In addition to the blue plaque on the wall of Hogarth House, the sculpture of the writer seated on a bench is to be located on the terraces near to Richmond bridge, a popular tourist spot. This will no doubt engender further celebrations of Virginia's life and work in years to come. Virginia wrote some of her most important work in Richmond, and her contribution to literature both as an individual and through her work with Leonard at the Hogarth Press, will finally be honoured with this beautiful artwork.

To support the project or for more information, go to: www.aurorametro.org

Beyond the Literary

> Beautiful statues have a look not seen on living faces,
> or but rarely, as of serene immutability.[3]

It is important to note that Virginia Woolf has left a lasting legacy, not only for her contribution to modern literature, but in other aspects of her life as well. She is widely recognised as an LGBT+ icon through her apparent bisexuality and her most famous love affair with Vita Sackville-West. It has now become common knowledge that Virginia had intimacy issues with her husband Leonard, but formed a close bond with Vita, also known as Mrs Harold Nicolson. It has been suggested that Virginia was a lesbian and used her marriage to Leonard to partially conceal the fact. People have differing opinions about this, but the fact remains that Virginia was willing to flout conventions and to write and publish about same-sex relationships long before it was fashionable to do so. She has been celebrated as part of LGBT+ History month mainly for her love affair and for the novel *Orlando*, which is regarded as the greatest love letter to Vita, and was inspired by Vita herself.

Through her personal writing, Virginia was very open about her mental health problems too, when it was largely a taboo subject, and this has helped to allow mental health to become more visible and to lessen the stigma attached to it. Ultimately, her mental instability resulted in her death, but her diaries and letters document her struggle, and they demonstrate that those suffering with mental health issues can achieve success and happiness. As Virginia writes in her final letters to Leonard, she had been happy and enjoyed a wonderful life; her death was the result of not wanting to impose on Leonard any further.

One important aspect of Virginia's life which is often overlooked, is that she is a sexual abuse survivor. Abused by both of her half-brothers, George and Gerald Duckworth, albeit reluctantly, Virginia allowed Gerald to publish some of her work, but later bought back the rights. In *Sketch of the Past* and *22 Hyde Park Gate*, she writes very honestly and openly about the abuse she suffered, once more allowing sexual abuse to be visible and to enable discussion.

In *A Room of One's Own*, Virginia writes about the freedoms of women to write, although fighting against the power that men held over women. This, of course, developed from two speeches she made to undergraduates at Cambridge University and is now often studied by literature students. This is widely regarded as Virginia Woolf's seminal work and as a great feminist text. It is mainly through this that Virginia has become known as one of the greatest feminist writers and much of the academic work inspired by Virginia focuses on the feminist aspect of her writing.

The vast amount of literature that has been inspired by Virginia Woolf is a true testament to her contribution to society and to British literature. There are dozens of biographies dedicated to her life, as well as her relationships with her family, friends and other great writers.

Earlier in this book, I mentioned that the book and film titled *The Hours* are both largely based on Virginia Woolf's writing. In 1983, her novel *To the Lighthouse* was adapted by Hugh Stoddart and directed by Colin Gregg as a film for BBC television which was nominated for a BAFTA. Her novel *Orlando* has also been adapted and performed as a play and director Sally Potter was inspired to make a film adaptation of the novel starring Tilda Swinton in 1992. *Mrs Dalloway* has similarly been adapted into a play and Eileen Atkins wrote the screenplay for a 1997 film version, directed by Marleen Gorris, and starring Vanessa Redgrave in the title role. A film titled *Vita and Virginia,* based on Eileen Atkins' play of the same title, and directed by Chanya Button, was premiered in Canada in 2018.

The numerous art works inspired by Virginia's life and work demonstrate her living legacy among current artists, writers and filmmakers, and we hope that they continue to inspire many more interpretations.

For a decade there has also been a competiton for women novelists in her honour – The Virginia Prize for Fiction – organized by Richmond-based independent publisher, Aurora Metro Books, also the publisher of this book.

There is no doubt that Virginia Woolf was one of the major literary figures of the twentieth century and for that reason alone, she deserves to be honoured as one of Britain's truly great women writers. As we hope this book has demonstrated, the town of Richmond played a significant part in her journey.

Recommended Reading

Bell, Quentin. *Virginia Woolf: A Biography* (London: Pimlico, 1996)

Dunn, Jane. *Virginia Woolf and Vanessa Bell: A Very Close Conspiracy* (London: Virago Press, 2000)

Evans, Margaret. *Virginia Woolf and the Hogarth Press in Richmond* (London: Richmond Local History Society, 1991)

Goldman, Jane. *The Cambridge Introduction to Virginia Woolf* (Cambridge: Cambridge University Press, 2006)

Gordon, Lyndall. *Virginia Woolf: A Writer's Life* (London: Virago Press, 2006)

Harris, Alexandra. *Virginia Woolf* (London: Thames & Hudson, 2011)

Holtby, Winifred. *Virginia Woolf: A Critical Memoir* (United Kingdom: Albion Press, 1988)

Hussey, Mark. *Virginia Woolf: A-Z* (New York: Facts on File, 1995)

Kennedy, Richard. *A Boy at the Hogarth Press* (London: Hesperus Press, 2011)

King, James. *Virginia Woolf* (London: Hamish Hamilton, 1994)

Lee, Hermione. *Virginia Woolf* (London: Vintage, 1997)

Light, Alison. *Mrs Woolf and the Servants* (Ldn:Penguin, 2007)

Poole, Roger. *The Unknown Virginia Woolf* (Cambridge: Cambridge University Press, 1978)

Porter, David H. *Virginia Woolf and the Hogarth Press: Riding a Great Horse* (London: Cecil Woolf Publishers, 2004)

Sackville-West, *Vita and Woolf, Virginia. The Letters*, Louise DeSalvo and Mitchell Leaska (eds) (San Francisco: Cleis Press, 1984)

Spalding, Frances. *Virginia Woolf: Art, Life and Vision* (London: National Portrait Gallery, 2014)

Woolf, Leonard. *Sowing: An Autobiography of the Years 1880-1904* (New York: Harcourt Brace Jovanovitch, 1960)

Growing: An Autobiography of the Years 1904-1911 (New York: Harcourt Brace Jovanovitch, 1962)

Beginning Again: An Autobiography of the Years 1911-1918 (New York: Harcourt Brace Jovanovitch, 1963)

Downhill All the Way: An Autobiography of the Years 1919-1939 (New York: Harcourt Brace Jovanovitch, 1967)

The Journey not the Arrival Matters: An Autobiography of the Years 1939-1969 (New York: Harcourt Brace Jovanovitch, 1970)

Woolf, Virginia. *The Letters: Vol. 1: The Flight of the Mind 1888-1912*, Nigel Nicolson and Joanne Trautmann (eds) (London: Chatto & Windus, 1975)

The Letters: Vol. 2: The Question of Things Happening 1912-1922, Nigel Nicolson and Joanne Trautmann (eds) (London: Chatto & Windus, 1976)

The Letters: Vol. 3: A Change of Perspective 1923-1928, Nigel Nicolson and Joanne Trautmann (eds) (London: Chatto & Windus, 1977)

The Letters: Vol. 4: A Reflection of the Other Person 1929-1931, Nigel Nicolson and Joanne Trautmann (eds) (London: Chatto & Windus, 1978)

The Letters: Vol. 5: The Sickle Side of the Moon 1932-1935, Nigel Nicolson and Joanne Trautmann (eds) (London: Chatto & Windus, 1979)

The Letters: Vol. 6: Leave the Letters till we're Dead 1936-1941, Nigel Nicolson and Joanne Trautmann (eds) (London: Chatto & Windus, 1980)

The Diary of Virginia Woolf, Vol. 1: 1915-1919, Anne Olivier Bell (ed.) (London: The Hogarth Press, 1977)

The Diary of Virginia Woolf, Vol. 2: 1920-1924, Anne Olivier Bell (ed.) (London: The Hogarth Press, 1978)

The Diary of Virginia Woolf, Vol. 3: 1925-1930, Anne Olivier Bell (ed.) (London: The Hogarth Press, 1980)

The Diary of Virginia Woolf, Vol. 4: 1931-1935, Anne Olivier Bell (ed.) (London: The Hogarth Press, 1982)

The Diary of Virginia Woolf, Vol. 5: 1936-1941, Anne Olivier Bell (ed.) (London: The Hogarth Press, 1984)

A Passionate Apprentice: The Early Journals 1897-1909, Mitchell A, Leaska (ed.) (London: The Hogarth Press, 1990)

Moments of Being: Autobiographical Writings, Jeanne Schulkind (ed.) (London: Pimlico, 2002)

A Writer's Diary, Leonard Woolf (ed.) (New York: Houghton Mifflin Harcourt, 1953)

The Voyage Out (London: Duckworth, 1915)

Night and Day (London: Duckworth, 1919)

Jacob's Room (London: The Hogarth Press, 1922)

Mrs Dalloway (London: The Hogarth Press, 1925)

To the Lighthouse (London: The Hogarth Press, 1927)

Orlando (London: The Hogarth Press, 1928)

A Room of One's Own (Ldn: The Hogarth Press, 1929)

The Waves (London: The Hogarth Press, 1931)

Flush (London: The Hogarth Press, 1933)

The Years (London: The Hogarth Press, 1937)

Roger Fry: A Biography (Ldn: The Hogarth Press, 1940)

Between the Acts (London: The Hogarth Press, 1941)

Woolf, Virginia & Haddon, Mark. *Two Stories* (London: The Hogarth Press, 2017) A reformation of the first Hogarth Press publication, with Woolf's story, *The Mark on the Wall* and Haddon's *St Brides Bay*. Includes a portrait of Woolf by Haddon.

Endnotes

Introduction

1 *Diaries I*:124

2 *Jacob's Room*:3

3 *Downhill All the Way*:11

4 *Beginning Again*:235

5 *Letters II*:150

6 *Beginning Again*:253

7 *Beginning Again*:254

8 *Diaries II*:13

9 *Downhill All the Way*:68

10 *Diaries V*:137

11 *Downhill All the Way*:52

12 *Downhill All the Way*:55

13 *Downhill All the Way*:9

14 *Diaries II*:187

Virginia's Richmond

1 *Beginning Again*:170

2 *Diaries I*:35

3 *Diaries I*:15

4 *Diaries I*:18

5 *Diaries I*:4

6 *Diaries I*:9

7 *Diaries I*:31

8 *Diaries II*:249

9 *Downhill All the Way*:11

10 *Diaries II*:285

11 *Diaries I*:304

12 *Diaries II*:295

13 *Diaries I*:13

The Hogarth Press

1 *Downhill All the Way*:27

2 *Beginning Again*:234

3 *Beginning Again*:234

4 *Beginning Again*:236

5 *Beginning Again*:236

6 *Diaries I*:61

7 *Beginning Again*:239

8 *Letters II*:255

9 *Diaries I*:218

10 *Beginning Again*:241

11 *Downhill All the Way*:6

12 *Downhill All the Way*:68

13 *Diaries II*:232

14 *Downhill All the Way*:64-65

Woolf on Writing

1 *Kew Gardens* in *A Haunted House: The Complete Shorter Fiction,* Vintage Classic Editions, 2003:85

2 *Diaries I*:229

3 *Diaries I*:271

4 *Diaries I*:266

5 *Night and Day*, Vintage Edition, 2000:315

6 *Night and Day*, Vintage Edition, 2000:316

7 *Diaries I*:307

8 *Downhill All the Way*:17

9 *Downhill All the Way*:61

10 *Letters II*:400

11 *Downhill All the Way*:59

12 *Diaries II*:28

13 *Diaries II*:106

14 *Diaries II*:111/112

15 *Jacob's Room,* Oxford's World Classics, 1999:129

16 *Mrs Dalloway in Bond Street* in *A Haunted House: The Complete Shorter Fiction*, Vintage Classic Editions, 2003:146

17 *Mrs Dalloway,* Oxford Classics Edition, 2000:3

18 *Letters VI*:212

Family in the Richmond Era

1 *Reminiscences* in *Moments of Being*:11

2 *Sketch of the Past* in *Moments of Being*:96

3 *Sketch of the Past* in *Moments of Being*:122

4 *Letters I*:129

5 *Letters IV*:390

6 *Reminiscences* in *Moments of Being*:26

7 *Sketch of the Past* in *Moments of Being*:126

8 *Letters I*:279

9 Dunn:144

10 *Letters II*:458

11 *Letters III*:493

12 *Letters II*:144

13 *Sketch of the Past* in *Moments of Being*:131

14 *Letters I*:257

15 *Diaries I*:282

16 *Diaries II*:242

17 *Old Bloomsbury* in *Moments of Being*:44

18 *Diaries I*:161

Virginia and her Servants

1 Light:2007:10

2 Light:2007:11

3 *Sketch of the Past* in *Moments of Being*,:105/106

4 *Diaries I*:5

5 *Letters II*:164

6 *Letters II*:214

Gatherings with Woolf

1 *Diaries I*:110

2 *Diaries III*:32

3 *Diaries II*:209

Health

1 *Downhill All the Way*:153

2 Hermione Lee, *Virginia Woolf*:164

3 *Beginning Again*:150

4 Hermione Lee, *Virginia Woolf*:184

5 Hermione Lee, *Virginia Woolf*:184

6 *Letters I*:428

7 *Beginning Again*:81

8 *Diaries V*:24

Virginia at her Leisure

1 *Sketch of the Past* in *Moments of Being*:133

2 *Beginning Again*:57

3 *Downhill All the Way*:14

Woolf on War

1 *Letters II*:76

2 *The War from the Street* in *Virginia Woolf: The Complete Works*, A to Z Classics Edition, 2017

3 *Jacob's Room*, Oxford World Classics Edition, 2000:246

4 *To the Lighthouse*, Oxford World Classics Edition, 2000:181

5 *Beginning Again*:179

Leonard's Viewpoint

1 *Downhill All the Way*:9

2 *Beginning Again*:28

3 *Downhill All the Way*:49

4 *Beginning Again*:170

5 *Beginning Again*:171

6 *Downhill All the Way*:10/11

7 *Beginning Again*:172

8 *Beginning Again*:176/177

9 *Beginning Again*:231

10 *Beginning Again*:235

11 *Beginning Again*:232

12 *Downhill All the Way*:52

13 *Beginning Again*:256

14 *Downhill All the Way*:15/16

15 *Downhill All the Way*:58/59

16 *Downhill All the Way*:98

17 *Downhill All the Way*:99

18 *Downhill All the Way*:117/118

19 *Downhill All the Way*:27

20 *Downhill All the Way*:14

21 *Downhill All the Way*:64

A Lasting Legacy

1 *A Passionate Apprentice*, written in Greece, 1906

2 *London Revisited Review*, 1916

3 *A Passionate Apprentice*, written in Greece, 1906

Index

Symbols

A

B

INDEX

T

For more great books go to
www.aurorametro.com